An Owl
Before Dusk

by Michio Nagai
Minister of Education, Science, and Culture in Japan

With an introduction
by David Riesman

---

*Fourth in a series of essays sponsored by
The Carnegie Commission on Higher Education*

The Carnegie Commission on Higher Education,
2150 Shattuck Avenue, Berkeley, California 94704,
has sponsored preparation of this report as part
of a continuing effort to obtain and present
significant information for public discussion.
The views expressed are those of the author.

AN OWL BEFORE DUSK

Library of Congress catalog card number 75-23937

Contents

Foreword

Written by Michio Nagai when he was an editorial writer for the *Asahi Shimbun* press and lecturer in higher education at Tokyo University, this perceptive essay stresses the interactions of education and the world's condition from perspectives of both Japan and the United States. The essay's title and theme come from Hegel's contention that, thus far in human experience, philosophy has been useful in defining and understanding forces and events only after they have taken nearly their full course. In Hegel's phrase, "The owl of Minerva begins its flight when dusk is falling" (Hegel, 1820). Nagai's theme is that somehow we must learn to anticipate and to alter our futures and now just to accept them when they come. And he believes that education, and particularly higher education, holds the key to that achievement.

The essay begins with a second avian allusion — to the death of canaries prior to mine explosions — and Nagai suggests that the troubled colleges and universities of the world might, like the canaries, foretell impending world disaster. His first chapter elaborates that theme from the viewpoint of the youth who become college and university students and who, in many nations, hold skeptical, often cynical views of the world. The second chapter describes the world condition from Nagai's own point of view. The role of universities, at what he describes as the current "turning point in world history," is defined in the next chapter as twofold: (1) to bring about a well-balanced industrial society in which there is sufficient diversity of ideas and (2) to redesign the industrial society to cope with problems brought about by changes at the national, international, and global levels. Nagai analyzes these roles largely in the context of Japanese experience, but the implications for the United States and other countries are clear.

In a chapter that analyzes the American system of higher education, he notes as distinctive the comparatively strong position of administrators in our educational institutions, the force of specialization in shaping our curricula and academic structures, the impacts of mass access to higher education, and the consequences for higher education brought about by efforts to provide services to the community. He then identifies several problems and contradictions in American higher education, calling attention, for example, to conflicts between the practical vs. the transformational approach to change, and to the tensions between nationalism and internationalism in the intellectual orientations of Americans.

The essay concludes with six proposals. In brief they are:

1 That organized skepticism should be the first principle of all education
2 That the education of tomorrow must be engaged in the exploration of the "inner frontier" of man
3 That the content of education should be truly international
4 That liberal education must be reemphasized
5 That diversity of education should be encouraged
6 That solutions to the general problems all peoples confront together must be considered more and more seriously.

The Carnegie Commission on Higher Education is pleased to publish this essay by a leader of education who is highly respected not only in his own country but internationally as well. Nagai knows the United States as student and as teacher, and he now has more influence over education in Japan than has any other single individual. As both an observer of and a participant in higher education in these two great nations, he has been in a unique position to study, to reflect, and to act. Whether the impending doom of industrial civilization is as threatening as Nagai indicates, or the potential solution (better education) as powerful as he suggests, only history will tell. But we greatly appreciate the wisdom he has shared with us, hopefully *before* the twilight of our opportunities to make a difference. If we do find ourselves located in the span of time still "before dusk" and if the "owl of Minerva" can reflect best within and speak most effectively through higher education, then the burden on and the challenge to the universities of the industrial world are indeed great.

We also appreciate the extended introductory essay by David Riesman, whose knowledge of American higher education is not only unsurpassed, but not even closely matched by anyone else, and who has been such a perceptive and appreciative observer of Japan — as Nagai has been of the United States.

Clark Kerr
Chairman
Carnegie Commission
on Higher Education

Introduction

Clark Kerr, as chairman of the Carnegie Commission on Higher Education, not only presided over a diversified group of men and women who, in the course of six years, issued a variety of reports as official Commission documents, but also set in motion a series of investigations into many specific, often quite technical, features of American higher education. These studies helped educate the Commissioners and, in addition, provided the largest and most comprehensive series of examinations of American higher education ever conducted. One of the most imaginative ideas of this enterprise was to ask some talented non-American observers to write reports dealing in some fashion with American higher education; it was taken for granted that the countries of origin of these scholars would provide reference points for comparison.

Just as there is inevitably a projective element in the views individuals have of each other, there are also such views among classes and ethnic groups and nations: If a Frenchman as brilliant and knowledgeable as Alain Touraine (1974) writes about American higher education, he will also write something by implication—and in this case explicitly—about the contemporary state of French higher education, on whose vicissitudes, both in the famous *Evénements de Mai* in 1968 and more recently, he is a leading authority. Similarly, in the succinct survey by Joseph Ben-David (1971), *American Higher Education: Directions Old and New*, we Americans can see ourselves more sympathetically than we are inclined to portray ourselves in our present state of disillusion with higher education. For Ben-David recognizes that some of the very aspects of American higher education we criticize, such as departmentalism, have also been a source of entrepreneurial energy and opportunity denied to the more chair-bound systems of centralized European countries such as France and Germany. Sir Eric Ashby's *Any Person, Any Study: An Essay on American Higher Education* (1970), like his other writing on "non-U.S." and non-U.K. universities, shows both his knowledge of American higher education outside the major world-class institutions, and his sympathy for open access rather than the more donnish attitude: "more means worse."

Michio Nagai's book is the most recent contribution to this sub-series, and from it we can learn a good deal concerning Japanese higher education and its relation to the total society—themes potentially illu-minative for the American scene.

I want to emphasize that process of transfer because both Western and Japanese scholars commonly speak of Japanese culture as "imita-tive," a judgment which Michio Nagai shares in some measure, although far less so than others in his general cultural milieu.[1] For the very notion of the book takes for granted, as few Japanese have done, that they have something to teach Americans (other than Zen Buddhism, which, as one Japanese told me a good many years ago, will come to Japan, if ever, through America!). A more sympathetic observer might say instead that the Japanese are "open" and "receptive" or have a great gift for syncretism—quite at odds, for example, with the French tradition (which Touraine combats in his life and work) which insists on an almost self-sealing autonomous culture (more like the Chinese than the Japanese) which would have much to contribute to the rest of the world if only the rest of the world were not so borné.

Each of these authors in the Carnegie subseries has had extensive experience of the United States, but of them, only Michio Nagai took his Ph.D. here—at Ohio State University. The benefits of that location are evident in his discussion of "The Education Manager," written on his return from the United States to Japan in 1953 and found in the pages that follow. Michio Nagai had the advantage of working with some particularly evocative teachers in sociology and anthropology at Ohio State, as well as cooperating on a project studying the fate of Western-educated intellectuals and academics after they returned to Japan and other countries in Asia. But he was also, as I would see it, spared the kind of provincialism of the visiting student or scholar who concentrates at the major university centers of the East and West coasts, with perhaps exceptions for Michigan or Chicago.[2] Since Ohio State is a land-grant institution, with a large college of education, Michio Nagai was exposed to a side of America which few Japanese saw at the time

[1] At a talk ten years ago at the Annual Asian Studies meetings, I criticized the unwillingness of Americans resident in Japan and at home there "to allow the Japanese to be different. . . . They wanted always to press the Japanese to learn where they stood, and they encountered vagueness, a kind of fuzzy quality which offended their definitions of rationality—definitions that sometimes equate ra-tionality with what is merely rationalistic." See "Japanese intellectuals—and Americans" (1964-65, p. 61).

[2] I once sought to make the same point to a distinguished graduate of a small private college, thinking to compliment him by saying it was advantageous for him to come from an eminent Japanese family to this midwestern college. Perhaps because of Brahmin snobbery or because both in the Japanese and American systems of academic invidiousness, the institution lacks distinction, at first he did not appreciate my remark!

or since; living already in what is the border part of a southern frontier that runs across Ohio, Indiana, and Illinois, he ventured even further South during his student days in spite of warnings that as a nonwhite person he might be subject to harassment and difficulty. Had Michio Nagai done his graduate work at, let us say, Princeton, or Yale, or MIT, he would have become alerted only with difficulty to the managerial emphasis in educational administration and to the separate career lines of school principals and superintendents and "ordinary" teachers. Like many more recent critics, Nagai comments (p. 25) on "the fact that society has given the status of directing education not to the long-haired great thinkers, but rather to the managerial types. . . ." While it is common to make sport of "educationists" at elite institutions, it is not common to understand their actual training and the trajectory of their careers. Yet one can read, almost with nostalgia, Nagai's 1953 observation (p. 24): "Along with considerable recreation, students—from elementary school through college—study diligently following schedules scrupulously prepared for them by the educational administrators. . . . The result is that if one compares American university students with their Japanese counterparts, the former are indescribably busy; if a student is idle for even a day, it is only with great difficulty that he will be able to catch up on his studies. For one hour of lecture, three hours of preparation and review are the standard."

Nagai's 1953 critical comments of doctoral programs in home economics, journalism, or photography, will fall on ready ears among devotees of the liberal arts. In recent years, specialization has had a bad name both among many devotees of high culture who regard only directly career-linked studies as specialized, and not their own subject matter, and among many upper-middle-class students who can often move directly from the *Cornell Daily Sun* or the *Columbia Spectator* or the *Harvard Crimson* into major metropolitan journalism without the need for (or the benefit of) a school of journalism—although photography among these same students might now be regarded an okay topic. Such readers would probably agree in principle with Nagai's comment that American destiny cannot be confined within America, but is influenced by the feelings of Africans, Japanese, or "Hong Kong coolies." However, with the dropping of foreign language requirements at graduate and undergraduate levels and in the high schools as well, many young Americans who regard themselves as cosmopolitan appear to me increasingly "domesticated." Non-Americans are expected to learn enough English to make love or do other business with American young people who now so readily go overseas on charter flights. Ironically, these young Americans, less ethnocentric than they were in Nagai's student days, commonly look at non-American cultures with a new respect, even envy, as one outgrowth of their new-found tendency toward self-disparagement of America—only to discover that many of the values they themselves have rejected are still eagerly sought by the less affluent and still only partially industrialized nations (just as these same values are still pursued by the not-yet-arrived within the United States).

In this connection, the beginning of Nagai's essay is particularly revealing because it reports a study "On Thinking of the Young People of the World" not widely known in the United States. It was commissioned by the Japanese Prime Minister's office, and involved surveying youth from 18 to 24 in 11 countries and finding virtually omnipresent a cynicism about the future, and one's own institution, about education both in terms of its supposed stifling of creativity and in terms of its usefulness in occupational advancement. (Like Nagai, I found it surprising that Swiss young people were so pessimistic about their own country's future.) The difficulty I have in dealing with such cross-national data is the lack of breakdowns by sex, social class, or ethnic groups within each country; for example, I would suppose that women are more peace-minded than men not only in the United States but elsewhere as well. Furthermore, in the data presented in this volume, the measures of intensity that Gallup and other able pollers often use are missing, so that we do not know whether, for example, we are dealing with a flippant surface cynicism, deep fatalism, or destructive nihilism, or various combinations of these.[3]

Like many observers of the student revolts in the late 1960s, Nagai sees the leaders of dissent as well as youth itself as a leadership class, showing their elders the evils of the war in Vietnam, pollution, materialism, and so forth. This is so commonly stated, here and elsewhere, that it is taken as history and considered true by many, whether or not they share the attitudes the young people expressed in their demonstrations. Nagai suggests, for example, that young people are worried about the dangers of nuclear explosion. Many were at one time, more in the United States and in Japan than anywhere else, for obvious reasons and not so obvious ones. But during the anti-Vietnam war agitation, I found it impossible to mobilize more than peripheral interest in questions of nuclear disarmament among activist college students or their faculty sponsors and mentors.

There is a danger, which Michio Nagai has not escaped and which I have not always escaped either, of reading into student protests our own values and beliefs, whether about university reform or societal

---

[3]For one of the most penetrating surveys of American opinion in this age group, see Yankelovich (1974), who shows the extent to which hostility to authority of the affluent has spread since 1969 to large numbers of working-class and noncollege youth, although, in the specific instance of the women's liberation movement, there would seem to remain a fairly sharp class dichotomy (as well as a racial one).

reform—much as left-wing intellectuals earlier read their beliefs into the actions and occasional expressions of the so-called proletariat. Hence, it is important to remind ourselves that it was not the young in the United States who discovered either the evils of war in general, especially nuclear war, or the Vietnam war in particular. Church groups (notably the Friends, of whom Nagai speaks in connection with Earlham College, a strong center of internationalism and peace activity); many Methodist and Catholic peace groups; organized women's groups, such as Women's International League for Peace and Freedom; natural and social scientists concerned with nuclear issues (some clustered around the *Bulletin of the Atomic Scientists*); journalists such as the late Bernard Fall and François Sully, who knew Vietnam; and, contrary to legend, some military, CIA, Rand Corporation and other so-called defense intellectuals, saw the dangers of war in Vietnam as well as nuclear war and the possible relations between the two before college students were alert even on the elite campuses, let alone in the country as a whole.

A greatly distinguished Japanese social scientist, to whom both the author of this book and the author of this introduction are devoted, has emphasized the importance of expressivity itself in the Japanese student movements, of camaraderie, and collective action often for its own sake; he has said this with sympathy in spite of the fact that, as an early, hence "premature" man of the moderate and scholarly left, he was, like his counterparts in this country and elsewhere, a chief target of the student extremists. And indeed, it is not right to speak simply of "student extremists," or of the "student movements," for in every case there were adult mentors, some of them brushed aside in the end, others following along, still others leading the way. While the generational breaks are sharp, as the poll data show, I think it is an historical error to judge that the students acted without adult leadership, even though it is also correct to assert that they helped create and recreate that leadership as the various movements developed.

However, Nagai and I do not differ at all in believing, on the basis of poll data (and our respective impressions), that students today are quiescent but not acquiescent; indeed, even the degree of quiet can be exaggerated, since disturbances which occur on the less visible campuses (such as violence in the spring of 1974 at Ohio University in Athens) or demonstrations at Salem State College in Massachusetts, or Boston State College, no longer make headlines or the national television circuits which, as Nagai emphasizes toward the end of this volume, play an increasing role in directing the moral traffic of Americans.

None of this is meant to suggest that I consider Nagai's criticisms either of Japanese or American higher education to be unfounded, only that I do not take the student protests at face value. The problem always remains as to what to put in the place, for example, of the system of examinations which the Japanese find so oppressive, so dehydrating for young people, so unresponsive to individual talents. Nagai himself would seem to argue at one point in favor of what Ralph Turner calls sponsored rather than contest mobility, when he notices that all five Japanese Nobel Prize winners were educated before the democratization of Japanese higher education that took place after the Second World War, but he elsewhere uses the word "elitism" in its now common pejorative meaning and is clearly on the side of open access and free competition.[4]

Nagai is realistic in seeing that higher education lacks the leverage for the enormous changes he believes are required if we are to live on Spaceship Earth as an harmonious family of nations. He sees the counterculture as, in part, a reflection of the awareness of dissident students in active revolt against the prevailing economy and society as no longer viable; he terms them "moderate social disorganizers" (p. 37). (One could add that, by dropping out of the race for high achievement, some upper-class devotees of the counterculture may make a bit of room in a stagnant job market for the continuing circulation of elites.)

And yet, despite such skeptical realism, Nagai also gives his essay a title that suggests greater hope for education: an owl before rather than after sunset. I agree with him. I think ideas are of immense importance though they are as apt to come from religious leaders or nonacademic intellectuals and artists as from universities. Consider the slogan of "the domino theory" as an illustration of an idea that had considerable power in supporting the war in Vietnam along with older American evangelism about bringing democracy and enlightenment to the supposedly "backward" people of Asia. The idea of progress itself was immensely influential: Nagai shares contemporary skepticism about "progress" and "development," although according to him such notions are not dead in Hawaii (however moribund they may be on the East Coast of the United States). Nagai himself has been a leading proponent of the concept of One World, even though he also recognizes the complex dialectic between nationalism and internationalism. Like other Japanese, he fears that nations armed with nuclear weapons can end life on the planet.

[4]The endless discussion about testing reminds me of a discussion with the Japan Teachers' Union leaders who, when I asked them what they would put in the place of the examination system, responded that the recommendations of school principals would be better, quite unaware of the even more "elitist" consequences of such a policy, or of the protection tests provided against pressures from principals or parents. (I might add that I believe tests could and should be developed to take account of a wider range of noncognitive qualities, but that is a long story; friends at Educational Testing Service are skeptical about the possibility of developing efficiently reliable projective tests for pertinacity, capacity to endure frustration, relative absence of narcissism, etc.). For a report on a discussion with the teacher's union officials, see Riesman and Riesman (1967, pp. 335 et seq.).

Nagai's American encounters, in Hawaii and elsewhere, remind him that what Americans often call internationalism is actually a vision of the world as becoming more like the United States. But he is also aware that for many cosmopolitan Americans, this is anything but a happy omen since the United States is seen by them, in an inversion of traditional chauvinism, as contaminating the rest of the world with its corporate and even with its philanthropic enterprises. It is in fact one of the virtues of Michio Nagai's book that he appreciates the heterogeneity of American higher education. For example, unlike most highly educated non-Americans, he is aware of the importance in the United States of the small, private liberal arts colleges, such as Earlham, Oberlin, Antioch, or Grinnell, which have had long-standing interest in deprovincializing students by exposing them to alien turf abroad or at home. Similarly, he is aware of the little theatres and off-Broadway performances away from all Broadways of America. Unlike what I would assume to be the judgment of most American readers, he has a good word to say for Robert Hutchins' idea of a college based on the Great Books, East and West. As he says (p. 44), "In the United States, therefore, the public policy of financing small but valuable educational experiments is desirable to maintain and strengthen the American tradition of diversity in education."

In my own judgment, though some students and faculty think otherwise, smallness per se is not a value; but the gigantism of some institutions takes them beyond the span of control even of those educational managers whose training Nagai observed at Ohio State University. However, it is possible to sustain diversity even in the great public institutions, as illustrated in Michigan by the three subcolleges of Michigan State University; by Oakland University with its subcolleges; subcolleges of Grand Valley State College; and by the Residential College, an experimental college within the University of Michigan. Similarly, at the University of California at Santa Cruz, the colleges would seem to be of manageable scale (600 students each) and to possess a certain architectural and cultural, if not always curricular, cohesiveness. To be sure, all such experiments in the public sector suffer from egalitarian pressures both within each institution and among them, since almost inevitably the costs on a per student basis of these subcolleges are greater than the costs in the community colleges; and the funding formulae established to give greater support to postbaccalaureate education is no help here. These pressures are intensified by the increasing demands of state legislators and state coordinating councils for budgetary accountability, along with the pressure for intrastate equity among institutions suffering from stationary or even declining enrollment.

However, in comparison with the relatively growing public sector, it is the bleak prospect of private higher education in America that most threatens our valued diversity. Major eminent, mostly Ivy-League, universities are surviving even in the face of budgetary deficits, in part because they can depend on tuition paid by or on behalf of students who seek the defensively useful credential they provide: a Stanford or Princeton baccalaureate degree seems worth saving, getting, and spending for. In contrast, even the Oberlins, Carletons, Earlhams, and Grinnells may suffer as students prefer, with the growth of "child liberation," not to burden their parents with the high tuition of private higher education, as tuitions rise along with hedonism and as students and parents alike are less willing to make sacrifices in the face of an uncertain future.[5]

Nothing could be more dramatic than the contrast Nagai points to of the situation of private higher education in Japan, which now enrolls 80 percent of the students, compared with 20 percent or less in the United States. Because until recently there has been almost no increase in the number of government universities, the vast expansion of Japanese higher education has taken place in the private sector, where honest administrators and shady entrepreneurs alike have been caught in an inflationary spiral which has led them to charge staggeringly large tuitions and often, as in the private medical and dental schools, entrance fees which are little better than bribes. Yet student-faculty ratios even in such eminent private universities as Keio and Waseda are by American standards unbelievably high; and it is not only the prestige and lack of tuition charges but also the more favorable student-faculty ratio which lead Japanese young people to endure what Ezra Vogel has termed "the infernal examination system"[6] to get into the leading public universities.

[5]The states are not likely to subsidize tuition in private colleges in much of the country where private education is a tiny minority and has no moral or political hegemony such as it does in parts of the Northeast, nor is the federal government likely to aid high-cost private colleges by sufficient subsidies to students of modest income and modest ability. I still think, as I have for many years, and as Christopher Jencks and I argued in *The Academic Revolution* (1968), that something like a Federal Education Opportunity Bank would allow students to borrow for their educational costs and pay back these funds, not through (often uncollectable) loans, but through the Internal Revenue Service, helping subsidize lowinterest rates and administrative costs if they strike it rich whether in real estate or in social science, while having the federal government share the burden if they strike it poor in social work or in the arts or in other fields where college-educated people seek "meaningful" but not necessarily remunerative work.

[6]See Vogel (1963). On the mushroom growth of private higher education in Japan, see Cummings (1973); and for a fuller discussion see Cummings, "The Politics and Prospects of the Japanese University," in a volume as yet untitled and unpublished, edited by Hugh Patrick and Lewis Austin. While, of course, Keio, Waseda, Doshisha, and other leading private universities do have entrance examinations, many junior colleges for women and other private colleges profit from the spillover of those who failed examinations or avoided them, thus providing a kind of "open access" based on the Japanese faith in education, and till the other day, the notable capacity of Japanese to accumulate savings. In this situation, as Cummings notes, the Japanese government is beginning to come to the aid of the private institutions, hard hit, as are the families themselves, by mounting inflation.

There is another respect in which Nagai's American experience, beginning at Ohio State and most recently at the East-West Center of the University of Hawaii, allows him fully to appreciate the inevitable and increasing ethnic diversity and the impact of this on American higher education. What many Americans see as a problem, namely, how to reconcile our ethnic and racial nationalism and ethnocentrism, Nagai sees as also an opportunity for the model of One World, which is the vision to which he keeps returning.[7] And it is here that he places particularly heavy bets on higher education in helping the students become less unfamiliar with the world outside the classroom, whether in the local neighborhood or in the World neighborhood. He recognizes, as many American educational reformers do not, that unsupervised field work in the local or the global village can be merely an anti-intellectual junket. He is notable for his desire to see faculty as well as students take stop-out or sabbatical periods prior to or during their university careers in which they engage themselves with some aspect of society outside the academic world. It seems to me possible that Nagai takes too much for granted what a Westerner like myself respects, namely, the ability of the Japanese school system to bring virtually the entire population to a reasonably high level of literacy in comparison with that in the United States—even though he also sees this literacy as frittered away in looking at television rather than in serious reading; and he emphasizes the cost in creativity of the stressful, relatively unified school system prior to university entrance. Indeed, precisely because of traditions of American anti-intellectualism, both old and "macho" and new and countercultural, there may be a greater danger in the United States than in Japan that the "real world" will be regarded as excluding the academic world, a notion which might have surprised Woodrow Wilson.

There are in fact, as Nagai knows, many experiments in extramural or even lifelong education now under way in American higher education. Many of the older departmental bulkheads and cultural boundaries have been assailed and weakened. Indeed, this is true in the study of history itself, which Nagai criticizes in his concluding pages as not comparable to the level of American natural sciences, although, in fact, historians have been working with oral history, census data, and other nonarchival materials in France, the United Kingdom, and the United States for a number of years now, and with a good deal of intellectual éclat. Still, it does not follow that American students become familiar with advances in the field of history when the general education that Nagai saw in 1953 as a virtue of the American colleges has become

---

[7]For a reflective commentary on how one can reconcile increasing pressures from white and nonwhite ethnic and racial groups in the United States on ethnic history and ethnic studies in the schools with some sense of America as a pluralistic nation among nations, see Glazer (1974, pp. 55-59).

attenuated as requirements disappear—although it should be added that there is a certain revival of interest in history as part of the swing away by many students from the cult of supposedly contemporary relevance.

That cult, however, seems likely to be one element in the similarity of attitudes turned up in the Gallup Poll commissioned by the Japanese Prime Minister's office with whose findings Nagai's book begins. Reading these and similar findings, I am sometimes tempted to think that it has become everywhere chic to say that one is alienated, almost as if aristocratic vices along with aristocratic liberations have become democratized! Of course, some of the same rock stars are popular everywhere, and some of the same sports, television dramas, and antinomian impulses. Each country's youth subcultures draw support both from diverse strata within each nation, as our white affluent youth often imitated what they thought to be proletarian blacks (not realizing that there are still many people in the United States who prefer to be called Negroes), while from Prague to Tokyo students learn protest tactics from each other—and often majored in sociology!

Still, I owe my initial interest in Japan to curiosity about a society which had industrialized by a different route from that of the West. While many Japanese themselves—like Americans at the East-West Center whom Nagai rightly criticizes—often tend to confuse "Westernization" with "modernization," I am skeptical of convergence theories; and I question the proposition that technology is making the whole world more alike, though not the proposition that it is making it more explosive and dangerous. The attitudes expressed in the Gallup Poll by Japanese youth are in percentage terms similar to those expressed, for example, in the United States. But each attitude is relevant to its own context, and has to be seen in terms of the expectations created locally as well as internationally.

I can illustrate by an example in Nagai's account of Japanese higher education which should be of interest in American readers, namely, the very small proportion of postbaccalaureate graduate students. It is something like 3 percent in Japan as against 12 percent in the United States. What an enormous difference that makes, even if one assumes that the Japanese high schools prepare most of their students better than American high schools do. It makes a difference for undergraduate education, robbing the Japanese of the mixed blessings of the TA, the teaching assistant, who acts as an intellectual and cultural middleman (should we say "middleperson"?) between faculty and college students. It limits the base of the pyramid on which the achievements of American research universities have been built.[8] It means that Japan is much less of a second-chance country than the United States, everything depends on one's undergraduate college in Japan, whereas in the United States, there are even third chances through a postdoctorate or through reentry into higher education at a later stage in life. Just as Tocqueville observed that Americans could go bankrupt and start over again without complete loss of face and legitimacy, so Americans even if their point of origin is lowly, can start in one college, transfer to another, drop out, stop out, complete their baccalaureate later and go on to graduate school, provided that they do well in the Graduate Record Examinations, or if, as is now often the case, graduate schools are underenrolled and hungry for students. Thus there is still a much greater looseness in the United States, as Nagai recognizes, than in a homogeneous society like Japan. This is our opportunity as individuals, and our danger as a country, for it leads to an anarchic individualism, and makes it seem almost impossible to imagine Americans enduring with civility, let alone equanimity and generosity, the austerities of the ecological prospect Nagai takes for granted. I continue to believe that Americans have much to learn from Japanese society: to the degree that Nagai's book talks about that society and its educational system, it should add to our illumination. And because Nagai's exposure to American higher education can begin with the base line of his memoirs of 1953, he helps provide the sort of perspective on the United States then and now which was Clark Kerr's hope in commissioning this set of volumes.

David Riesman

[8]It is clear from the Carnegie Commission subseries that the American research university with its undergraduate college or colleges and its combination of research, graduate training, and undergraduate teaching, is relatively unique. Much Japanese research goes on, as also with us, in private industry or in institutes funded by industry, or loosely linked to government universities. The great expansion in the private universities has occurred in the relatively "cheap" fields of the humanities and the social sciences, just as with us; law schools have expanded and newly opened up to accommodate the flood of postbaccalaureate students who, in my judgment, often mistakenly hope in this fashion to discover economic security, personal autonomy, meaningful and even socially useful work—for law schools are cheap to start and staff and, at the worst, their three-year programs serve to postpone entry into an uncertain occupational world.

Acknowledgments

It was in 1968 that Dr. Clark Kerr first asked me to write an essay on higher education in the United States on the basis of my experiences and observations. I was glad to comply, for he generously urged me to express candidly and critically my ideas on American higher education.

Because of the great changes in my life that followed my decision in 1970 to give up my post as a university professor and become an editorial writer, my usual working habits were upset, and the writing of this essay was consequently delayed. I wish to express my sincere gratitude to Dr. Kerr for his patience, as well as for the foreword he has kindly written for this book.

Dr. David Riesman, from whom I have learned so much in the past, has written a lengthy introduction to my essay, serving once again as a kind teacher whose words illuminate and clarify what his student has wished to say.

In the process of writing and rewriting my essay, I have received valuable suggestions and kind assistance from Mr. Verne A. Stadtman and Miss Karen Seriguchi of the Carnegie Council on Policy Studies in Higher Education, Professor Yoshio Hara of the Tokyo Institute of Technology, Miss Sharon Minichiello of the University of Hawaii, Miss Patricia Murray and Mr. Tsutomu Kano of *The Japan Interpreter,* and Miss Yasuko Aramaki of the *Asahi Evening News.* I am indebted to all these friends.

I should like to note that this essay was written while I was an editorial writer for the *Asahi Shimbun,* before my appointment as Minister of Education, Science and Culture on December 9, 1974.

Michio Nagai

June 1975

1. The Thinking of Young People

It is said that before the explosion of a mine, a canary falls down. The university disturbances in advanced industrial societies in the latter half of the 1960s seem to have been somewhat similar phenomena.

After the Second World War, two superpowers — the United States and the Soviet Union — entered a period of competition; there was conflict and tension between them and between surrounding nations, some directly and others indirectly allied with either of the two. Though there are distinct differences between the two systems, one based on Marxian socialism and the other on free-world thought, there have been clear similarities in their emphasis on the importance of the masses, high specialization, and social competition combined with the division of labor.

The educational explosion took place against the background of the competition of these two systems and affected nursery schools to graduate schools. Education and research developed within governments and industries. Lifelong learning became common in many parts of the world. Consequently, the breadth of education — not only in the United States and other advanced nations, but also in emerging nations — is now beyond comparison with what it was before the Second World War.

Another turning point has been the precipitous development of communications media in the 1960s. If printing can be considered the first revolution in the field of communication, the second would be the utilization of electric telecommunication in the nineteenth century, and the third would be the progress of electronics, which made possible the diffusion of television and computers.

Ironically, when technological innovation and the educational explosion reached their peaks, certain negative effects of industrialization became apparent. There were university disturbances. People began to suffer from pollution, energy crises, and alienation in large social organizations. Man was also threatened by the possibility of a third world war — a fear that has not dissipated since the end of the Second

1

World War. Students who participated in university disturbances have not clearly conceptualized these problems, but they seem to have felt the difficulties and even the crises of civilization, and, in expressing their doubts and desires, have used methods that were sometimes violent and illegal. The use of such words as *progress, development, growth,* and *evolution* have been taken for granted during the two centuries since the Industrial Revolution in the West — and in Japan, for approximately one century since the emergence of a modern state during the Meiji Restoration. In recent years, such words have been subject to severe scrutiny, not only by students, but also throughout other sectors of the population, including the older generation.

The most important problem for education, including higher education, during the 1970s and the following years will be whether it will be able to deal with the doubts and questions students have raised since the latter half of the 1960s.

On the surface, the universities are far more quiet today than they were during the late 1960s. To be sure, radical students remain active, though in a more sporadic fashion, in such nations as West Germany and Japan. These students, however, seem to have become more involved in off-campus matters, dealing not with university problems, but with what they regard as social evils.

Are the students who are quietly studying on the campuses really satisfied with the world about them, or are they leading lives with anxiety deep in their hearts? In the autumn of 1972, the office of the Prime Minister of Japan conducted a study on the thinking of young people in the world. The office spent approximately $220,000 and asked the Gallup organization to survey young people of 11 different nations: six nations from Europe (the United Kingdom, France, West Germany, Sweden, Switzerland, and Yugoslavia); two from the Americas (the United States and Brazil); and three from Asia (India, the Philippines, and Japan). Young people between the ages of 18 and 24 were questioned.

The survey included 29 major questions, which in turn were broken down into smaller parts. The areas of study, six in all, were family life, school life, occupational life, friends and leisure, national and social life, and views of life. A report based on this study (Sorifu, 1973), was published in July of 1973. In general, the study found that the youth of the world are neither satisfied nor confident with regard to the present-day situation, and they are pessimistic about the future.

It is not possible to elaborate on the study here, but two points are relevant to our present concern. The first is that there is more common thinking among the youth of highly-developed societies, extending across Europe, the United States, and Japan, than among the 11 nations of the survey as a whole. The second point is that although there is common thinking among the youth of these highly developed nations, the Japanese reflect somewhat more pessimism and dissatisfaction than is evidenced among the Americans and Europeans.

SIGNS OF
OMMON DIS-
TISFACTION

Young people today are dissatisfied about education, society, and politics, and are pessimistic about the future of the world. The study included the statement: "Present-day schools tend to evaluate students merely on the basis of examination results and give little attention to their human qualities." Japanese and Westerners responded nearly the same way — 71.4 percent of Japanese, over 70 percent of young people in the nations of Europe, and 67.9 percent of the Americans agreed with the statement. Another statement read, "Schools tend to place too much emphasis on the mere memorization of knowledge at the cost of creativity." Again, the responses of these nations were nearly the same. It has been a belief in Japan that Japanese education overemphasizes memorization in contrast to the Western emphasis on creativity; according to the study, however, young people elsewhere feel the same way about their own education — 72.3 percent of British youth agreed with the statement in contrast to the slightly lower figure of 63 percent for the Japanese. Americans and Europeans other than British were not very different from either one of these two groups.

It has also been a belief that teachers in Japanese schools and universities have been relatively mechanical in the methods and content of their teaching. Again, the study found that 70.9 percent of the Americans agreed with the statement: "Many teachers try to communicate their knowledge mechanically." The Japanese response — 61.8 percent — was slightly lower, not only as compared with the American response, but also to the British, Swiss, and Swedish responses.

Why do young people go on to advanced schooling? Because they want to receive more education, or because they want to prepare the way for a more profitable professional career and marriage? Do they merely want to satisfy the wishes of their parents. . .or do they go because others are going? Young people of different nations continue their education for very similar reasons. Among the nations of the free world, more Americans (43.2 percent) think that further education will improve their chances for success in career and marriage. This percentage of Americans was, however, lower than the percentage of the only socialist nation in this study — namely 48.9 percent for Yugoslavia. The Japanese percentage — 39.4 percent — was higher than those of the other European nations, but lower than Yugoslavia's.

Educators throughout the world have been claiming recently that student self-government and student participation in university governance are and should be major trends in education. Responding to the statement that "Schools do not reflect the opinions of pupils and students," the majority of American and Swedish youth disagreed, thus indicating that the young people of these two countries are satisfied with their representation in schools.

To summarize the above points, young people of industrialized nations today do not think that their school life, including higher, secondary, and primary education, is quite satisfactory. School is not felt to encourage creativity and freedom of young people; instead, teachers are believed to teach mechanically and to force students to learn by memorization. Furthermore, students themselves tend to view schools as social ladders they must climb for a successful career and marriage.

Is humanity more respected in the larger society? Young people do not think so. Eighty percent of the Swiss, 66 percent of the Japanese, and 61.7 percent of the Americans agreed with a statement that "The company nowadays places too heavy an emphasis on profits and does not pay much attention to the effects of its activities on people." In their responses to the statement: "In the present grossly materialistic society, money reigns supreme," young people seem to be seriously cynical about the economic growth of today. Between 80 and 90 percent of the young people questioned in the three countries of Japan, the United States, and France thought that present-day society was materialistic.

But even if people live under conditions in which neither school nor business life is satisfactory, people might be appeased to some extent if politics were functioning properly. Here again, however, to the statement, "The government sometimes goes in the opposite direction from that in which the people really want it to go," more than 80 percent of the young people in Japan, the United Kingdom, the United States, and Sweden gave an affirmative answer. It is said that we have come to the end of a materialistic era, and that governments are paying increasing attention to individual human rights within the nation and to cooperation and solidarity in international relations. Unfortunately, young people do not think that present-day politics are performing such functions, as is shown by responses to the statement: "The government is placing too much emphasis on the benefits of the nation as a whole at the cost of individuals." With the exception of those in West Germany, the majority of youth in all of the industrialized nations agreed with this statement.

Indirect, or representative, democracy, which we know as parliamentary government, was established in Britain from the latter half of the seventeenth century to the beginning of the eighteenth century. The establishment of this type of government, however, did not solve all of society's problems — a situation that gave rise to several revolutionary theories in Europe from the end of the eighteenth century on. At the same time, however, there were thinkers who took the position that it was possible to carry out social reform without recourse to revolutionary means. To do so, they believed it was necessary to use methods of direct action, such as demonstrations and strikes. One famous thinker who took this position in Britain in the 1930s was Harold Laski.

After World War II, the principles popularized by Laski became widespread, and by the 1960s, his views were strongly advocated in many countries. Today, a rather small number of youth feel that parliamentary governments in most of the industrially advanced countries have effective channels for expressing protest or dissatisfaction. Fewer than 40 percent felt so in the United States, France, and Switzerland; only 50 percent felt so in Japan, the United Kingdom, West Germany, Sweden, and the Philippines; and only a little over 40 percent indicated so in India and Brazil.

When parliamentary governments (indirect, or representative democracy) offer insufficient means of protest, there is no other course than to resort to methods of positive and direct action, such as lawful demonstrations and strikes. Fifty percent of the young people surveyed in the United States and Switzerland, and around 40 percent in Japan, the United Kingdom, France, Sweden, and India regard such alternatives as necessary. When even these methods do not produce results, the young feel that they must resort to illegal means, such as violence, or to giving up and dropping out of society. In West Germany, France, and India, over 6 percent felt the use of illegal means was acceptable under such circumstances. Of the Japanese youth questioned on this point, only 3.6 percent — a fairly low percentage — approved of resorting to violence or to other illegal means.

As for giving up and dropping out of society, 40 percent of the young people questioned in Brazil said they would opt for this method of protest over violence or other illegal means. The percentage of Japanese youth subscribing to this viewpoint was comparatively low — only 4.8 percent would opt for this way of protesting when other methods failed.

We can see that the use of methods of protest built into the British model of parliamentary government is now giving way to the combined use of methods from the parliamentary model and direct action.

The greatest problem in the matter of protest today is how to handle the combination. The key to rebuilding future society is for groups such as students and unions to express their opinions by means of lawful strikes and demonstrations, and for politicians and business people to listen to them sensitively, taking their complaints into serious consideration. Otherwise, illegal means, such as violence, will increase, or we shall see more young people withdrawing and dropping out, leaving society to stagnate.

Indirect action through parliamentary government is acceptable to young people if they feel they can really entrust politics to suitable persons by means of election. However, it is a bad situation when young people go along with the system simply because there is no other way of getting things done or when they feel powerless as individuals to reform politics. Seventy-three percent of the young people in Japan stated as their reason for relying on indirect democracy the inability of the individual to effect desired political reforms. This rate is overwhelmingly high compared with other countries of the world, and indicates that Japanese youth are not very positive about protest.

It is not surprising that another finding of this study was that young people seem to believe that their society is mired in bureaucratic routine. One statement was specifically addressed to this point: "Present-day society is an unhappy one because men in organizations perform their assigned jobs mechanically." More than 70 percent of the Japanese and Americans regard this as the case.

It is not too difficult to infer on the basis of the survey by the office of the Prime Minister of Japan that young people are pessimistic about the future. To the statement, "We will have a better society to live in 30 years from now," only 28.5 percent of the Japanese agreed. A greater percentage of Americans (40.4) gave an affirmative response but the majority remained negative. Eighty-one percent of the Swiss were also negative.

Since the end of the Second World War, many throughout the world have longed for the end of the arms race in order to avoid a third world war, and in connection with this, the question was asked: "Is human wisdom capable of avoiding a world war?" In answer, 34.3 percent of the Japanese said "no," and it is alarming that 62 percent of the young people from Switzerland, a nation that has been struggling for world peace by adhering to a neutralist position for years in the heart of Europe, do not think that a third world war can be avoided. The negative responses from the United States and the United Kingdom were also in the majority.

In politics, journalism, and education today, there is widespread discussion about pollution. The study asked, "Is human wisdom capable of doing away with pollution?" Again, 55.6 percent of the young people of Switzerland, a country known for its scenic beauty, responded that it is not possible to do away with pollution. Americans and other Europeans showed the same trend, averaging about 44 percent. Young people from the one socialist state included in the study, Yugoslavia, were more optimistic, with only 28.6 percent giving a pessimistic response. For Japan, which has been known as a country with a high degree of pollution since the United Nations Conference on Human Environment in Stockholm in June, 1972, the percentage of young people who are pessimistic was 47.7 percent, which followed only the Swiss.

It may be, then, that in 1974, universities in advanced nations look quiet. If the present study can be relied on as some measure of the thinking of young people, however, this tranquility must be regarded as merely a surface phenomenon. It also has been assumed that advanced nations are the ones where the quality of life and the wisdom of man are also advanced. The study shows, however, that young people seriously doubt this assumption, and one is forced to say that the volcano of student dissent that erupted in the latter half of the sixties is now quiet, but not dead.

DISTINCT
ACTERISTICS
HE JAPANESE

Let me now proceed to the second major finding of the study — that the Japanese exhibit characteristics that are distinctly different from those of the Westerners. Generally speaking, Japanese people are more dissatisfied and anxiety-ridden than their Western counterparts. Two members of the office of the Prime Minister, Tamotsu Sengoku and Atsuko Toyama, co-authored a book entitled *A Comparative Study of Japanese* (1973) which was based on this survey. They made two interesting points. The first was that Japanese young people are more tradition-oriented in their thinking. The second point, interestingly enough, was that Japanese — more so than Westerners — are driven by severe daily competition. When these two characteristics are combined, uniquely Japanese thinking is bound to appear.

The study by Sengoku and Toyama shows that the young people of Japan have a far stronger sense of belonging to their families, companies, and school groups than do Westerners. These characteristics have been often pointed out by both Japanese and non-Japanese scholars, such as Ruth Benedict (1946), Chie Nakane (1972), Masao Maruyama (1963), and Takeyoshi Kawashima (1950). The percentage of young people who form a conjugal family is far smaller in Japan than in the West and the frequency of moving from one job to another is also far lower in Japan. Even in the age bracket of 18 to 24, those Japanese who are married but still live in an extended-family setup comprise 29 percent. In Sweden, the percentage is 2.5 percent and in other Western nations, with the exception of Western Germany and Yugoslavia, less than 10 percent. Of course, the Japanese percentage should not be explained solely in terms of traditional consciousness vis-à-vis family life, for occupational mobility is extremely high in the United States — even in the 18- to 24- year age bracket — with 28 percent of the respondents having changed their jobs four times. This is in sharp contrast to 2.7 percent in Japan, a far lower figure, not only than that of the United States, but also of other European nations — with the exception of Yugoslavia.

Japanese seem to think that friends should have a sibling, or parent-child relationship. For the statement, "One should get deeply involved in the affairs of friends," 68.8 percent of the Japanese agreed. This attitude may be somewhat difficult for Westerners to understand; only 12.1 percent of the French, for example, thought as the Japanese do on this question. Here, Americans are more similar to Japanese than to any other Westerners, with 44.5 percent agreeing with the statement.

If present-day Japanese society were still the stagnant, agrarian society it once was, the sense of familial loyalty exemplified by the Japanese respondents would be quite suitable. The fact is, however, that Japanese today are living in a rapidly changing industrial society in which the agrarian population comprises less than 20 percent of all categories of the gainfully employed population. Scholars in and outside of Japan point out that the secret of Japan's rapid economic growth can be explained to a great degree by the Japanese tradition-oriented sense of loyalty to enterprises, to the government, and to the whole nation. Not only is it true that a business enterprise acts like a large family, but a school also tends to take on the characteristics of an enclosed society. In addition, all these schools and enterprises are ranked into a class order within the total social system. Under such arrangements, each enterprise is forced to compete with other enterprises (and each school with other schools) as a family unit. In a rather curious way, therefore, the traditional group solidarity of Japan has bolstered the acceleration of social competition in the sphere of education and business.

It is not at all surprising that such negative effects as pollution and city problems of all kinds have been brought about quickly in Japan by the most rapid rate of economic growth and industrial change in the world. One must look, however, into the other conditions that made the Japanese case somewhat unique. The country is small, with about 80 percent of its area being mountainous; it is also short on resources. In addition, Japanese industrialization moved on under the monocentric guidance and sponsorship of the government in Tokyo. The combination of these elements was helpful in bringing about rapid economic growth; unfortunately, it also invited negative effects.

Finally, one of the most interesting things the study showed was that many young people in Japan today think that human nature is inherently bad. It has long been said that religions of the Far East have regarded human nature as inherently good, in contrast to Christian thinking, which fundamentally accepts the notion of sin. But to the statement, "Human nature is inherently bad," 33 percent of Japanese agreed, in comparison with approximately 20 percent of the British,

French, American and West Germans who also gave an affirmative response. Obviously, young Japanese, who used to think in a rather traditional way that the larger society, like a nation, should remain as a harmonious family, are now thinking that life in Japan has become too competitive. Accordingly, they seem to be reflecting such an attitude in their views of basic human nature.

2. A Turning Point in World History

Are the grievances of young people unwarranted? Have the young been indoctrinated by sensational mass media, or have they become victims of "soft education," acquiring, therefore, the tendency to express dissatisfaction rather than satisfaction?

Events in the 1970s seem to indicate that the serious concerns of young people today are not illusions. The youth are not always correct in their assessment of the contemporary situation nor in their predictions of the future; if they were always more perceptive than the older generation, there would be no need for education. When one looks at and considers the meaning of events in the seventies, however, one must take seriously the expressions of young people as shown in the survey discussed in Chapter 1.

Major happenings of the 1970s may be summarized under three categories — global, international, and national. Events at all three levels indicate that the 1970s are a turning point in world history.

BAL EVENTS   For the first time in human history, all mankind is now required to cooperate to solve concrete problems at the global level. In the spring of 1972, the Club of Rome published the report entitled *The Limits to Growth* (Meadows et al., 1972), which was followed in June of the same year by the UN Conference on Human Environment in Stockholm. *The Limits to Growth* warned the world that if five processes continue at the rate they have been proceeding, all growth will come to a complete stop within a century. The five processes are population growth, food production, depletion of natural resources, industrialization, and pollution. Some scholars argue that the report was much too simple in confining its discussion to those five processes. Even conceding that details of *The Limits to Growth* will have to be radically modified in the future, the fact remains that the report is attracting worldwide attention. In early December, 1970, an international conference at the California Institute of Technology had "The Future of Technology — Hopes and Fears," as its theme. It is inconceivable that a conference with this theme or a book entitled *The Limits to Growth* could have been widely received during the 1950s or even during the early 1960s, for the future of technology was then still regarded by most people with hope and with the belief that it would bring about endless growth. In fact, however, mankind had already been given an alarm. In August 1945, when the nuclear bomb was used to end the war, we saw what could have been regarded as the first symptom of a negative effect of technological innovation.

It has taken some years for all of us to begin to realize that we should not take too simplistic a view of growth and progress, and that we should be deeply concerned about current global problems. Religions of the East and West raised profound questions concerning the basic problems of mankind many centuries ago. Now, for the first time, the concerted voice of scientists is stimulating similar questioning with regard to man's destiny.

Global problems must be viewed in close relationship to international problems, in which epoch-making changes also took place during the initial period of the 1970s.

INTERNATIONAL EVENTS

In the autumn of 1971, the People's Republic of China — a nation with the largest population in the world and of a kind theretofore nonexistent in the history of modern states — joined the United Nations. In spite of its size, however, the government in Peking publicly announced that it belonged to the Third World, suggesting a similarity to the Third Estate of the French Revolution era. The emergence of the Third World itself, which includes not only China, but also approximately 100 nations all over the world, is an unprecedented phenomenon in the history of man.

The war in Vietnam came to a cease-fire in the early spring of 1973. At the end of the same year, Arab nations stood up with the slogan of "Resource Nationalism," which represented their independence and national interests in relation to the nations of the North.

These events, though seemingly separate, stem from the same root: these are the voices of the Third World asking for a readjustment of the relationship between North and South. In our solution of global problems, therefore, it will be necessary by all means for each nation of the North and of the South to find its proper role in relation to other nations. In the long run, there should be increasing cooperation and solidarity of people regardless of nationality. In order to achieve such a long-range end, it will be necessary to study closely the problems involved in international relations for the 1970s.

NATIONAL EVENTS

Against the background of global and international changes, each nation is bound to face drastic sociocultural transformation. Nations of the South will be more concerned with national sovereignty, economic prosperity, and the realization of national cooperation within the country. And because resources are limited and the human environment must be cherished, advanced nations in the North will become increasingly responsible for the preservation of resources and a healthy environment. Not only is lowering the rate of economic growth necessary, but also "zero growth" or even less will have to be considered seriously. In 1971, the United States declared a new economic policy in international relations, and at the conference for the International Monetary Fund during the same year, a decision was made to devalue the dollar. Since then, there seems to have been increasing friction and conflict in economic interests among more advanced nations. Here again, the long-range objective must be to work out stable cooperation among these nations rather than to increase discord.

To achieve this goal, it will be necessary to concern ourselves not only with the minor changes and readjustments in our present-day socioeconomic structures, but also to reflect deeply on the basic assumptions underlying the process of industrialization during the last two centuries. (It has been believed, for example, that limitless desire, production, and consumption is good). One must say that, for the first time since the Industrial Revolution, all of mankind in general is being forced to undertake such a task.

Events at all three levels today — global, international, and national — seem to suggest that we are now at an unprecedented turning point in history. This is not to say that science and technology should be abandoned. Instead, they should be used more wisely for human welfare. The expressions of young people in the survey discussed in Chapter I have not always been logical. But they must be considered in relationship to the drastic changes of our times. Furthermore, we must realize that no one, not even the world's leading intellectuals, has clearly understood the course of world history. Thus the task today of education in general, and higher education in particular, is to encourage students and teachers to work together to understand the rapidly changing historical context of their existence.

3. Two Major Tasks of Higher Education

Although they are not usually differentiated analytically in the thinking of young people, there seem to be two major tasks for higher education. The first is to bring about a well-balanced industrial society in which there is sufficient diversity of ideas. The second task is somewhat in conflict with the first: it is to redesign the industrial society of today to cope with problems brought about by historical changes on the three levels mentioned in Chapter 2 — national, international, and global. To put it more concretely, the second task of higher education is to build up a culture and society for a postindustrial age in an industrially advanced society itself.

In Japan, the nature of the difficult relationships between these two tasks seems to be clearer than it is in the United States. Japan embarked upon industrialization much later than the Western nations, including the United States, and had many difficulties as a backward nation. Consequently, the Japanese are still faced with concrete tasks in politics, business, and in the field of education. At the same time, the negative effects of industrialization are more clearly evident in Japan than they are in the Western world, with the result that Japanese are undergoing strong pressure to build up a culture and society for a postindustrial age for their sheer survival (Nagai, 1971).

Let me first point out problems that Japan, as a backward nation, has faced during the past 100 years. Although the leaders of Japan during the Meiji Restoration thought about alternatives for the future of the country, their final choice was crystallized in the famous slogan, "Wealthy Nation and Strong Army." "Strong Army" was dropped from the slogan with the defeat of the country in the Second World War, but "Wealthy Nation" has remained as a consistent key objective, only the wording has been replaced by the more modernistic phrase, *"economic growth."* In short, the most basic principle of politics, business, and education in Japan has been to catch up with the West in order to safeguard the independence of the country; and for the achievement of this goal, the Japanese have thought that national prosperity was indispensable. Education in Japan has been regarded under such circumstances as a means to achieve the national objective.

The Japanese have thought of at least four major methods to realize such an objective. The first — monocentric planning and control — is far more efficient than diversified initiatives and autonomy in local communities and independent organizations. The second — imitation of the West — has been a quick and sure way to achieve industrialization in the shortest time possible. This has been considered so important that the Japanese concentrated their efforts on such imitation at the expense of creativity. The third was the emphasis on practical education, which must be regarded as more important than liberal and cultural education when education is geared toward national economic prosperity. The fourth — equality — was upheld to a certain degree as an indispensable principle for the purpose of the mobilization of all the people in the nation. It was not given too much importance, however, for the combination of an elitist and mass social structure is a surer and quicker way of bringing about industrial changes. When these four policies are combined, the weaknesses of education in Japan are not too difficult to detect. Even at the present time, when Japan ranks as the nation with the third largest GNP, diversity of ideas is not encouraged in local communities and independent organizations. Japanese appear to be overly imitative and insufficiently creative. Although education at the primary and secondary levels has already spread to a great degree to all the population on an equal basis, the elitism of Meiji society is still evident in higher education. Moreover, in spite of Japan's rich cultural tradition, education today still strongly emphasizes practical orientation, at times too much at the expense of liberal and cultural education.

These four weaknesses are now clearly understood by most Japanese educators, including the Central Council for Education, which belongs to the Ministry of Education. They seem to agree that these weaknesses must be done away with if Japan is to come of age as a well-balanced industrial society that pays sufficient attention to welfare, equality, creativity, culture, nature, and internationalization. In other words, since the end of the Second World War, Japanese have regarded education in the United States as a model. About the end of the 1960s, however, when the Japanese began to realize the importance of overcoming these weaknesses in their own system, the model of education in the United States and in some other Western states began to lose its validity probably because of the changes that occurred in world history.

Looking at China as a close neighbor of Japan, it is inconceivable, for example, that its population of 800 million would drive automobiles as the Japanese do, for such a situation would not only suffocate the Chinese, but would also have an adverse effect on their neighbors and possibly mankind. It is also inconceivable that a large number of children in such a great state would compete from childhood for entrance by way of examination into the University of Peking as their Japanese counterparts compete to gain entrance into the University of Tokyo. If education in China were planned and controlled in the monocentric Japanese way, the whole nation would become much too bureaucratic. When these problems are so clearly evident, is there any excuse for the Japanese to maintain their present system of industrialization, which encourages every family to own an automobile and in which a great part of the population lives in the few large cities that offer better job opportunities and that give their children the best chances of succeeding within the Japanese educational system?

Under such circumstances, politics, business, and education in Japan are bound to consider seriously the idea that, rather than the expansion of the GNP and the raising of per capita income, a better quality of life somehow must be achieved. This is such a new way of thinking that no one in Japan, nor anywhere else in the world, knows how to approach a solution. Japanese are now caught in the dilemma of copying the educational achievements of the West and overcoming, at the same time, difficulties from which the Western nations are suffering.

Let me illustrate these points with reference to the historical changes Japan has experienced. The adeptness of the Japanese at imitation should be explained not so much in terms of national character, but rather by the historical role of which the Japanese have become conscious since the Meiji Restoration. Dr. Henry Dyer, a British scholar who taught at the Engineering College of Tokyo University in the 1870s, told his students that they should try to imitate the West for some years to come, even if they were deeply interested in creation, because the development of Japan at that stage made imitation necessary (Nagai, 1971). Interestingly enough, such thinking has been maintained to the present – even surviving the Second World War. One result is that, even though the GNP of Japan ranks third in the world, graduate schools in Japan are at a very backward stage. According to statistics of 1973, the number of graduate students in Japan was nearly 46,000, 3 percent of the number of undergraduates (Monbusho, 1974). In comparison, the number of graduate students in the United States in 1971 was already over 900,000, or 13 percent of the number of undergraduates (U.S. Office of Education, 1972). European higher education in this regard is more similar to the American system than to the Japanese. The number of graduate students in the United Kingdom was only 42,000 in 1970s, but the ratio to undergraduates was 22.6 percent. In France, also, the ratio of graduate students to undergraduates was 12.4 percent.

The reason the government and business in Japan have not been interested in the development of graduate schools may be explained in relation to national economic development. It has been far more profit-able for Japanese to buy patents from more advanced nations than to invest a large amount of money in the creative research of Japanese scholars and students. In addition, the purchase of patents has been a surer way for rapid industrialization.

The government of Japan, for the same two reasons, has been inter-ested in building a school system from the bottom up. In this sense, the design of the total educational structure is somewhat different from the one found among some emerging nations after the Second World War, wherein higher education developed faster than primary education. By 1900, 96 percent of Japanese were attending compulsory primary schools; during the 1920s and 1930s, the secondary schools were strengthened, and there was even the expansion of higher education to a certain degree. After the Second World War, educational expansion relied very heavily on the development of the private institution, for which the government did not have to spend even a penny until 1971.

If education is considered a vehicle that serves the blossoming of cultural creativity beyond economic prosperity, it may be said that Japanese education during the last century has stagnated at the level of the Dark Ages. An outstanding cultural historian of the West, Sir George B. Sansom, wrote in a preface to his work, *Japan—A Short Cultural History*, that Japanese culture had more universal values prior to the Meiji Restoration and that the culture since then has not been as great (Sansom, 1946).

This is not to say that there has been no effort among Japanese educators to build up schools that are independent from the govern-ment; but due to the processes of industrialization and the percentage of the masses in secondary and higher education, it has become in-creasingly difficult for private schools to maintain their respective inde-pendent values vis-à-vis the major national goals of a wealthy and strong nation. The process of imitation, increasing emphasis on practicality, and the homogenization of education has become even more intense in postwar Japan in which, constitutionally, there is supposed to be more emphasis on the freedom of individuals. The five Nobel Prize winners from Japan, three in science, one in literature, and one in politics, were all educated in prewar schools. The deterioration of private schools may be shown by abundant data. In 1974, the 968 institutions of higher education enrolled 1,900,000 students. The proportion of high school graduates going on to higher education is now 32.7 percent. However, 80 percent of the university population are attending private univer-sities, where there is a ratio of one teacher for every 31 students, in contrast to the teacher-student ratio of one to eight students in publicly supported universities. Furthermore, the physical space allotted for one student in a private university is one-third of the space allotted for a student in a public university. In addition, because government subsidies to private medical and dental schools have been meager, these institutions ask for large donations from the families of students as one of the entrance conditions. It is not at all rare for a family of a student to donate $70,000 to $100,000.

During the university disturbances in Japan in the late 1960s, the grievances of students were fairly specific: (1) Education below that of higher education had become too deeply involved in preparation for the university entrance examination — preparation that is necessitated by the fact that the majority of students wish to enter the good, but relatively few, publicly supported universities. (2) Because those who enter private medical and dental colleges must have a large amount of money, about 70 percent of them are children of private practitioners. Consequently, Japanese medical and dental education has abandoned the principle of public service. (3) All schools have been too deeply involved in the enhancement of the basic national policy of economic prosperity.

Given these conditions of higher education today, two major problems stand out very clearly. First, for the majority of Japanese, higher education of good quality is still closed. Second, as the case of the private medical and dental colleges shows, private institutions tend to be increasingly oriented to profit-making at the expense of the public interest. The remedy for such a situation is for the government to build up higher education through more subsidies. This is the only way to meet the need for equality in education and to reorganize the content of schooling in all school systems, which have so far neglected liberal education in their emphasis on entrance examination preparation. But even if such reforms could be achieved, education in Japan would remain far from ideal.

It will be necessary, by all means, for Japanese to redesign their own society for sheer survival. In 1973, the national bestseller was entitled *Japan Sinking* and sold over 3,000,000 copies. It is also noteworthy that every time there is a university disturbance in Japan, at least one group speaks of the importance of the cultural revolution in China, emphasizing the value of the agrarian commune and criticizing the evils of the bureaucratic entrance examination.

Education by itself will not be able to effect a new society. Politics and the economy will have to suffer also in order to find a new system in which human survival and dignity can be assured and in which greater possibilities for the happiness of man can be achieved.

4. Impressions of Higher Education in the United States in 1953

Fundamentally, higher education in the United States may face the same tasks as it does in Japan — although the first major task, that of building an industrial society that supports a diversity of ideas, is not of such serious proportions in the United States as it is in Japan.

Let me, at the outset, quote my first impressions of education in the United States as I recorded them in 1953 when I returned from the United States to Japan (Nagai, 1956).

Distinguishing Features of American Education

1. The Education 'Manager'

One of the noteworthy developments in American educational research is the branch of study called "educational administration." There are a great many people in the world of education called "specialists" who have received training in this field, and the educational administration studies of America, as well as this type of specialist, are quite different from those with which we are familiar in Japan. It would seem, therefore, that one of the keys to understanding American education is in this area.

Looking at the educational administration texts of Reeder, Mort, Lewis, and others, there appear first of all such sound arguments and eminent views as democratic ideals, the role of education in a democratic society, the fulfillment of the individual personality through education, and social progress. Following are explanations regarding the administrative setup of education in the federal government, states, counties and school districts, plus a commentary on legislation related to education.

To this point, it is rather conventional and similar to educational administration as we think of it in Japan. From here on, however, American educational administration studies generally, and to a remarkable degree, take on the character of educational management techniques: What type of control should the educational administrator have over teachers? What type of contact with parents? Which educational approach should one adopt in rearing individuals useful for the future?

The problems are not limited to these alone. There is thorough admiration for the "operations" sphere of this field of study.

Those who aim at becoming educational administrators generally are taught information necessary from an architectural standpoint – that is, lighting, ventilation and such matters related to the construction of a building. He must also have general knowledge regarding the mental health of students as well as the assembly halls, sports, recreation, dormitories and such which promote good mental health. Concern for the practice of management, in reality, goes into the greatest detail.

Looking at Reeder's book, for example, one finds "efficient" and "scientific" solutions for problems such as the selection of the fuel companies and the most useful way of negotiating to insure the best heating for winter, as well as the most practical route for school buses to take in dispatching students to their homes (Reeder, 1941).

In short, as the world of education from grade school through college in America today is considered to be similar to the operational system of a big company, it is treated in that way. The educational administrators are the managers of this educational enterprise; and educational administration studies for becoming a future "manager" can be undertaken for the first time upon entering graduate school.

To become a regular school teacher, that is, the "usual company employee," four years of college alone are adequate. The educational administrator, however, who launches on a career after having received a Ph.D. by completing three to five years of graduate school and acquiring the high-class, specialized knowledge imparted during that period, is, from the beginning, given completely different treatment from the usual company employee – the regular teacher. On becoming a public school teacher, the usual beginning annual salary is approximately $3,000; but for the new educational administration Ph.D., approximately $6,000. The pluses and minuses of American education can be better understood if one tries to think of them as related to the special characteristics of educational administrative studies and educational administrators.

Although the new Ph.D. in this field can start out at $6,000, he does not occupy a very prestigious position at the beginning. It would probably be the status of an elementary school principal, or, if he is fortunate, a dean of students in some small college. For that alone, there is a great number of Ph.D.s and the employment of a large number of educational managers. The result is that the educational management system of America is gigantic.

First employed, the new manager would not be too concerned with relaying to parents the lofty ideals of education. Living in a small cottage with his young wife, he becomes a member of the community's social set. To begin with, the great educational ideals, hopes of social progress and similar matters which are summarized quite briefly at the beginning of the educational administrative texts are rather self-evident. More than that, isn't one of the points stressed in these books that of becoming acquainted with the VIPs in the school's surrounding communities?

Thinking along these lines, he skillfully captures the attention of important people at PTA and school committee meetings through his clever jokes and fine sense of humor.

Still, he has even more important work to do. Is there good sunlight in each room? Is the flavor of the cafeteria soup up to par? Are the students' chairs at the correct height? What is the condition of the turf on the sports field? With no time to spare, his most important function as a manager directing this school operation is that of paying close attention to the physical plant and to human relations.

For example, suppose he finds the gymnasium unsatisfactory. Applying the whole store of knowledge gained during his years of schooling, and putting into practical use the most up-to-date information gathered from the specialist journal *Educational Administration* which he reads each month with deep interest, he carefully prepares a detailed plan for the construction of a gymnasium which is less expensive and, at the same time, more healthful and modern.

This plan is presented in the newspapers and at school board meetings, and people praise his up-to-date, specialized knowledge; he is considered a creditable scientific specialist and a manager qualified to be entrusted with administering the education operation.

In every issue of the journal for educational administration studies, there appears practical information from others like him who put scientific knowledge to use for the purpose of reforming the existing state of education — both its material and non-material aspects. This journal is also the arena in which educational administrators vie with each other in displaying their achievements; and after two or three of one's superior achievements become known through this publication, he will be pursued by other schools and school boards with offers of new positions at a yearly increase of $2,000 or $3,000 over his current salary.

In this way, the junior manager will probably become an intermediate, and, in due time, a senior manager; if he progresses as far as the position of superintendent of education in New York State, he is a big man drawing an annual salary of $48,000.

The result of the manager's importance having been recognized in educational circles is that recently a considerable number of universities have been appointing these specialists as university presidents instead of ex-scholars as was the former practice.

2. American Education Methods

According to the report of the American educational critic Benjamin Fine, Americans annually spend considerably more on tobacco than on education, and sacrifice for alcoholic beverages 2½ times that which they spend for education.

For many, therefore, it is difficult to take pride in American education, and while conscientious Americans, including Fine, feel a sense of shame, foreign critics use the actual situation as suitable material for heavy faultfinding.

However, this rationalized, efficient educational machine to which any number of educational managers have devoted all their energy is, when we foreigners first consider it, surprisingly fine and thorough. For those accustomed to the university libraries of Japan where one must search out books with the spirit of an explorer, the service of American libraries is a blessing.

In the same way, those accustomed to Japanese universities where student lounges are a rarity would likely be envious of the student lounges of American universities even equipped with blankets and beds which can be loaned out for naps.

There are beautiful universities in every state; and whether it be grade school or college, there is usually a fine lawn surrounding the buildings. Along with considerable recreation, students — from elementary school on through college — study diligently following schedules scrupulously prepared for them by the educational administrators.

Unlike Japanese universities, there are practically no students unaccounted for on the school registers. Initially, therefore, one should regard with respect the crystallization of the labors of these educational managers.

However, more than the fact that educational expenditures are limited (the matter with which Fine was concerned), the problem of American education is rather in the direction of the very enthusiastic outpouring of effort by the managerial group. In the first place, there is the problem of the amazing uniformity and standardization of education. However, American education is not under the direction of a central governing body like the convenient Ministry of Education in Japan. Local autonomy is to this day an important organizational principle; and uniformity in the United States is not obvious, but subtle.

The managers of the educational enterprise think of the education mechanism as something like a system where humans are mass-produced, and they are working constantly towards the rationalization and greater efficiency of mass-production methods.

One might say that this trend is even more obvious in American universities where educational administrators have diligently worked out for each block of study an efficient system stipulating preparation and review time, with an exam every one or two weeks. The result is that if one compares American university students with their Japanese counterparts the former are indescribably busy; if a student is idle for even a day, it is only with great difficulty that he will be able to catch up on his studies. For one hour of lecture, three hours of preparation and review are the standard.

Going out into the world after four years in this type of system, the average person is stereotyped and indoctrinated — but at the same time, well equipped with an adequate store of specialized knowledge.

Of course, American educational administrators also have recognized this type of danger (the risk of becoming a person devoted solely to conventionalized, specialized knowledge); and since the 1930s, they have been stressing the importance of general education along with specialization. The irony is, however, that this same general education which aims at liberating the human abilities, personality and ideals is also taught within the framework of the rigorous mass-production type of educational system through methods selected by the educational managers. For example, at Ohio State University, there is a subject called "Design for Living." Discussions about Plato, Shakespeare, and at times the *Ikebana* of Japan are the focus of this class — that is, topics which students in Japan pursue in rambling talk in coffee shops and student living quarters.

However, at the efficient American universities, subjects like this also count for three credits; and for each hour of class, three hours of preparation and review are required along with the exam every one or two weeks. One wonders what the meaning is in taking a test every one or two weeks in "Designs for Living."

The second problem for consideration is that these educational managers who studied briefly about democratic "thought" and quite thoroughly about the "skills" and "science" of management also devote to the education machine which they themselves control much more energy toward the areas of skills and science than to that of thought.

To begin with, the fact that society has given the status of directing education not to the long-haired great thinkers but rather to the managerial types within society is probably an indication of the keen appreciation of the idea that society itself is a body which requires scientific skills for advancement through the power of education rather than through wearisome thought.

Even the new state universities, possibly reflecting this type of social trend within American society, concentrate a surprising amount of energy on science and skills; and there are almost no branches of human activity not included in these special domains. There are even Ph.D.s in home economics; and there is very little these young ladies don't know about the types and operation of electric refrigerators and ovens.

It is somewhat difficult to imagine that there are Ph.D.s in journalism, sports, photography, etc. – and what is more, that these individual specialized areas are independent in the form of departments and curricula.

Turning out Ph.D.s with precise knowledge regarding the operation and types of scores – one might say hundreds – of cameras is probably necessary during present times when there continues to be an increasingly high degree of specialization, and is in itself not harmful.

However, when American educational managers engaged in this scientific, technical domain try to apply the same approach wholesale to human beings, society and the study of history, a blind spot in American education appears. The new education provides a good training in on-the-spot surveys and experimenting with one's ideas in actual practice through the natural sciences method – even for social phenomena; and such education is most likely useful in rearing experiment-minded, scientific people. However, the destiny of Americans today is influenced by the feelings of Africans who cannot always be seen by the eye or touched with the hand, and is swayed as well by the course of Japanese history and the happiness or unhappiness of Hong Kong coolies.

When occupied with such problems, Americans, who find it difficult to have confidence in a situation without actually seeing or feeling it, suddenly become captives of American mythology: "Our fate has always been to work for the ideal of democracy and the liberation of the human being . . ." and similar ideas.

Thirdly, one could talk on in detail about the ways in which education which is guided by technical managers tends easily toward maintenance of the status quo. It is a fact that there are beautiful schools in every state; but it is also a fact that if one makes a comparison of the federal states, the educational expenditures for a child in a Southern Negro school are approximately one-third of the usual. It is also a fact that according to an intelligence index for 100 youths, one out of every two persons above the average will go to college, while only one out of every eight below the average will be able to enter. It is evident that the problems of individual and class differences have not passed from American education, even with the coming of the age of automation.

Moreover, American education today probably should be more concerned with the ways of dealing with world problems. The fact that approximately 30,000 foreign scholars and students are involved in American universities does not in itself settle the problem.

It goes without saying that in the above space, I have only sketched out one of the very important special characteristics of American education. There are efforts everywhere to try to re-examine the ideals of democracy which are described briefly at the beginning of the educational administration texts, and to re-structure American education.

The future of that education will most likely be influenced by the extent to which these serious efforts can effectively compete with the power of the educational managers, and, on the other hand, according to the ways in which changes in the world situation and within American society act upon her educational system.

Looking back, I feel that there might have been some biases in my first impressions regarding American higher education. Living in Ohio and attending Ohio State University, I did not know the social climate and content of education and research in more established graduate schools on the East Coast and in some parts of the West Coast and the Midwest; nor did I know the strengths of the small liberal arts colleges all over the country. In addition, I came from the philosophy department of an elitist school in Japan where there was unusually little emphasis given to the occupational and pragmatic emphasis in education and research.

In fact, I wrote on the strength of small colleges in the United States in 1962, as follows:

One of the strengths of American culture is that in spite of the emphasis by Americans on the "big things," some "small things" have persisted throughout the history of the United States. Greenwich Village in New York has been known as a writers' and artists' compound, but it is also a place where there are many small theatres; and while staying in New York in 1960, I attended *Our Town* by Thornton Wilder and the *Threepenny Opera* by John Gay. In Japan, also, we have small theatres, such as the Actor's Theatre in the Roppongi section of Tokyo, but the difference is that small theatres in New York frequently have dramas which enjoy long runs of more than one year. There are at times long-run shows in Japan as well, but there has not been any which has continued for over one year. The reason the Japanese small theatres have this difficulty is very simple: the popular shows move on to large theatres or become movies due to the fact that large enterprises try to make money out of them.

American small theatres exist not only in New York, but in Chicago, San Francisco and other places as well, and I have been told that there are a sizable number of people, both actors and audiences, who are in support of these theatres. I am not an expert on theatrical activities, but I could not help thinking that the existence of such small theatres is a reflection of a facet of American civilization that is often missed even by many Americans — that is, that in addition to the famous large universities in many cities, there is also a large number of small colleges in the United States, spread throughout the country.

It is interesting to note that small liberal arts colleges do exist mostly outside cities; and the enrollment is usually less than 5,000 in these colleges, such as Amherst, Dartmouth, Antioch and Earlham. One of the reasons for this is that these colleges have developed originally out of churches located in local communities. In the case of Japan also, in the ninth century, there was such a university which developed along with a temple in the countryside at Mt. Koya, which is towards the south of Osaka. However, the Japanese people and policy-makers decided to break away from such a tradition at the time of the Meiji Restoration and, at the same time, defined the country as a "backward nation" vis-à-vis the industrialized Western states. The university accordingly became a symbol of modernization, industrialization, Westernization and urbanization; and the universities which have been built since Meiji are located in city areas. The size of these universities, on the whole, is as large as the city universities of Europe and the United States. In contrast to this Japanese trend, the United States and also European nation-states maintained small colleges, even during the period of industrialization — small colleges such as those at Oxford and Cambridge and at Heidelberg University, located along the beautiful Neckar River.

It is true that small liberal arts colleges in the United States are now a minority within the system of higher education; and because they are a minority, they seem to be resistant to and critical of current historical trends. In Richmond, Indiana, the population of which is less than 30,000, I visited a small college where I enjoyed giving lectures and also engaged in discussions with students. This college of modest means is based on the ideal of pacifism of the Quakers; and I found both the faculty members and the students to be rather critical of contemporary America. At the same time, however, they are the ones who are carrying on the American 'pioneer' tradition. A large number of students in that college are interested in African and Asian countries, and some of them are living in nations of those areas (Nagai, 1962).

However, it was true that I was amazed at the practical side of higher education and the close relationship between higher education and society in the United States. I was astounded also by the narrowness of specialization in a university like Ohio State, a narrowness that was linked to the structure of the division of labor in an industrial society. Although I mentioned that there was an element of conservatism in higher education in the United States, I did not feel that the problems in the relationships between the larger population and the minorities, especially blacks, would be so acute in the following years. In short, during my first stay in the United States, I felt that both the larger society and higher education had reached a well-balanced harmony.

In spite of these biases, the three problems mentioned in my article of 1953 — namely, homogeneity, overspecialization and conservatism — really did become far more acute in the 1960s during the period of the university disturbances than I had formerly anticipated.

5. Problems in American Higher Education

In a way, the 1960s was the decade in which American higher education reached its peak. Higher education of the European type was for the elite; the uniquely American kind of higher education, embodied in the idea of the land-grant college, was for the masses. And, in the 1960s, the United States realized to the highest degree in the world universal higher education. Accordingly, not only primary and secondary but also higher education began to exert great influence over the larger society. The idea of land-grant colleges, proposed by Senator Morrill roughly one hundred years ago in this new nation, was unprecedented in the history of higher education in the world.

It is commonly pointed out that the development of higher education in the United States is indebted to three different traditions. The first is the American tradition brought about initially by the establishment of land-grant colleges in the latter half of the nineteenth century. It emphasizes two objectives: (1) the diffusion of ideas to the largest possible number of people by opening wide the doors of the universities supported by federal and state governments and (2) providing, through research and education, practical services to the communities that surround universities.

The second is the German tradition of highly specialized research, first introduced, also in the latter half of the 19th century, in the graduate school of Johns Hopkins University. Here the emphasis was originally on truth for the sake of truth; but later on, the strong emphasis on specialized research began to be combined with the objectives of the first tradition.

The third is the British tradition of character-building through the learning of the classics. The emphasis here was somewhat contrary to the objectives of the land-grant movement. Universities were to become ivory towers cut off from daily concerns of the secular world. Many Eastern universities and small denominational colleges carried on this tradition. It is important to note, however, that this approach to education was to a large degree transformed when it was incorporated into the general education curriculum of larger universities in the twentieth century.

American higher education blends these different traditions in a unique way. It endeavors to perform a critical function, such as pointing out problems in the larger society. It assumes that its interests are global, transcending national interests, and that its mission is to advance the welfare for the many — wherever they may be — rather than small segments of the larger society. It also emphasizes the pursuit of truth for its own sake. In these objectives, the university differs from the society in which it exists.

At the same time, American higher education strives to be instrumental in bringing about rapid industrial development and economic growth in the larger society. It shows deep concern for the improvement of life in the communities that surround it. In this sense its concern can be directed to the interests of a small, local social unit within the nation-state. In this narrow sense of its mission, the "pursuit of truth" is often regarded as merely the self-centered activity of aloof scholars.

These two emphases — the practical and the critical — have been kept in balance most of the time thanks to the careful design of the university system. Three different branches of higher education develop and harmonize these different emphases: (1) a larger number of graduate schools have been established at least partly to enhance research; (2) various attempts have been made to initiate different types of general education for the purpose of character-building and of broadening man's knowledge of nature, society, and culture; and (3) a branch of professional and vocational education has been developed in order to prepare students for careers. Although most designers and administrators of higher education undoubtedly intended to keep a balance between practical and liberal education, the tradition of the land-grant colleges has become increasingly important during the rapid development of America's mass-oriented technological society. The fact that state-supported universities began to play a more and more important role in serving the technological society seems to prove this point. They have become so important in the post-World War II period that even prestigious Eastern private universities are not immune to their influences.

In addition, when the nation is faced with such crises as war, depression, and internal social disorder, its demands of higher education are bound to increase. During the economic setback of recent years, students themselves seem to have become more concerned over the employment situation than over international affairs.

Under such circumstances, balances between practical and liberal education cannot be maintained easily. As the practical side of higher education becomes stronger, those students and professors who believe that the objectives of universities derive from the traditional emphases on the welfare of mankind, the building of character, and the pursuit of truth become more dissatisfied.

I have pursued these issues with many students and faculty members — at Stanford University from 1967 to 1968 and at the East-West Center from 1972 to 1973. Many of them expressed deep concern over both domestic and international affairs, and have said that higher education today is not adequately performing its critical functions in order to bring about necessary reforms. One reason so many young Americans in the study discussed in Chapter 1 expressed dissatisfaction with their country may be explained partly by the deepening psychological conflicts in campus life today.

Ironically, however, when higher education has become part and parcel of the larger society, it cannot remain apart as an isolated institution; consequently, not only is it influenced by the politics and business of the larger society, but it is bound to share common ideals and ideas with the larger society. It is inconceivable that the 50 percent of college-age people who are enrolled in some form of higher education can be completely autonomous from the other 50 percent of the same age group. Otherwise, the whole society would be divided into sectors.

Let me here attempt to clarify a little more analytically the structural similarities between higher education and the liberal society. In the third chapter of his *Social Theory and Social Structure,* Robert Merton analyzed the relationship between science and the democratic order.[1] According to his argument, the development of science is enhanced in a certain social structure, and it seems that a democratic social order is the most suitable. He mentions four common structural characteristics of scientific endeavor and the democratic social order. The first is *universalism,* which, according to Merton, finds expression in the canon that truth claims are subjected to preestablished, impersonal criteria that are the same for all people. The second structural characteristic is the *communism of ideas,* according to which knowledge is not treated as individual property. Rather, any invention or discovery becomes the common property of all through the use of as open communication as possible. The third is *disinterestedness,* which requires people in education and research to be completely independent of any motivations. The fourth is an *organized skepticism,* a prerequisite for the pursuit of truth that is never absolute but always remains at the level of relativity, consequently making it necessary for people to be engaged in everlasting exploration. All these four principles apply both to organized scientific engagement and to the democratic social order.

---

[1]"Organized skepticism involves a latent questioning of certain bases of established routine, authority, vested procedures, and the realm of the 'sacred' generally" (Merton, 1964, p. 547).

Talcott Parsons discussed Merton's analysis in his comments on the structural characteristics of higher education in *The Social System* (1951), and he argues that there are five such characteristics in higher education. The first is *functional specificity,* according to which the scholarly interest of professors and students must be directed to some specialized subject rather than being diffused on many different problems. Second, Parsons also emphasizes the importance of universalism, and he defines the role of academics in terms of a universally valid cognitive generalization. Third, he discusses the importance of *achievement,* as opposed to judging people according to such ascribed qualities as sex, social class, or nationality. In higher education, any person must be evaluated on the basis of his or her performance rather than on an ascribed quality. Fourth, as Merton speaks of "organized skepticism" and "disinterestedness", Parsons discusses the importance of *neutrality of affection*, which means that in a scholarly society, emotional elements must be restrained as much as possible so as to achieve the calm and fair study of any subject matter. Fifth, he observes that *collectivity orientation* is more important than the individual for the enhancement of higher education. This seems to be similar to what Merton calls the "communism of ideas," in which the concept of the individual property of knowledge must always give priority to the common objective of the pursuit of knowledge for the benefit of all society.

The ideas proposed by these two sociologists apply even today to the analysis of higher education, and it seems that these structural characteristics are also applicable to the parliamentary system, journalism, and the occupational structure of the larger society. For example, in a highly developed occupational structure of the industrial type, the endeavor of any person must be evaluated by universalistic criteria, and such endeavor must be highly specialized within the framework of the division of labor. There also has to be the restraint of emotional behavior in occupational activities; and any achievement has to become the common property of all as soon as possible. In the larger society, there are other social groups, such as kinship, nation, race, or ethnic groups, that do not share these structural characteristics; but as the larger society moves more and more in the direction of an industrial type, the commonality of characteristics between higher education and the larger society becomes increasingly intense.

It is important to note that the value structures of higher education and the larger society show negative effects during the present period of radical social changes when the basic assumptions of these values are under strong pressures. In other words, these structural factors are resistant to radical sociocultural change in the following ways:

First, both in education and in the larger society, there is increasingly narrow specialization (characterized as "functional specificity" by Talcott Parsons). This means that if the person is engaged in a serious study in higher education today and turns out to be successful in a given occupational structure, there is a likelihood that he will lose sight of the overall problems of both the society and education. *Second,* the combination of the principles of achievement and universalism is also likely to cause almost any person to adhere to the present social order. The combination of the two accelerates competition; and when each person competes against all others, the solidarity of the people can be lost, with the result that they may be subject much too easily to manipulation by those in power in the larger society. In other words, people could be divided and ruled before realizing it if they are obsessed with the notion of "keeping up with the Joneses." *Third*, the highly industrialized society is structured according to the principle of the division of labor, as outlined by the French sociologist Emile Durkheim. It is a society somewhat like a carefully built solid skyscraper; its strength lies in its very bureaucratization. *Fourth,* one should not lose sight of the educational influence from various sources outside of the classroom, among which image communication on TV would be most important. Even before the diffusion of TV, David Riesman (1950) had discussed in his book *The Lonely Crowd* the "other-directedness" of contemporary man. When a person is exposed to commercialized TV from infancy, he is inclined to form the habit of unconsciously making adjustment to the rapidly changing great mechanism of the contemporary world. He is as quick as radar to detect the direction in which the system is moving, and as quick as a chameleon to change the color of his ideas. A person is now brought under the influence of TV before even primary school begins to exert some influence; but such a person is the most important input for school education, including higher education.

The most important resistant factor, however, seems to lie in the close relationship between higher education and the larger society itself. As I have emphasized repeatedly, higher education has become a part of the larger society, with the former influencing the latter. Nevertheless, the fact remains that the larger society is bound by politics, national sovereignty, and the national economy, and we are now living at a time when the national boundary of politico-economic activities must be relativized vis-à-vis the wishes of other nations. This is especially true and important for a nation that has a position of greater power and prosperity.

In addition, the larger society in such nations as Japan and the United States might have chosen, and still may choose, the wrong direction for development. Likewise, higher education in those nations might have been and still may be obliged to follow the same path, at least to a considerable degree. We are reminded that the direction of the larger society in industrially advanced nations today is under close examination due to the fact that mankind is faced with the global problems of resources, environment, population, food, and the like. The larger society itself will undoubtedly have to transform its direction in coming years.

As pointed out in Chapter 2, we are now confronted with a three-dimensional change in world history — that is, of global, national, and international dimensions. Under these circumstances, both the larger society and higher education in such nations as the United States and Japan must become truly international. But although it is easy to speak of this ideal, it is extremely difficult to put it into practice.

Between 1972 and 1973, I served as director of the Communication Institute of the East-West Center in Hawaii. In comparison to Japanese on the whole, a large number of Americans are far more internationally minded; there is, however, the peculiar problem that a fair number of Americans believe that internationalization is synonymous with Americanization.

My most recent stay corresponded with the period when the United States was muddling through the bitter efforts to end the Vietnam War. If her failure in that war could be attributed to her military intervention, why, then, did America intervene? It seems to me that the failure was due to overemphasizing Americanization with regard to Vietnam.

Carrying this argument further, some young staff at the East-West Center argued that Americans lack an understanding of autonomy, not only of Vietnam, but also of other nations in the Asian and Pacific areas. The idea that internationalization is synonymous with nationalization seems to be rooted deep in American tradition. The United States has a unique history in that it has succeeded in Americanizing immigrants with heterogeneous traditions. The country also has been successful in incorporating into the federation such diverse areas as the Republic of Texas, the French territory centered around Louisiana, and Hawaii. Christian evangelism and the diffusion of science and technology are also vital components of the American tradition, and these factors, too, have constituted the base for a conviction in Americanization and have helped to strengthen it.

Some Americans believe even today that there is the possibility of constructing a better world if they educate peoples in developing areas and help their development by satellite and other forms of communication. A good number of American people expect multinational enterprises to perform such a role. Many studies have already shown, however, that a strong sense of nationalism in developing areas is essential for the creation of a new international order; and the nature of nationalism is to accept Americanization and Westernization on the one hand, but to resist them on the other.

For nationalism often takes place in opposition to Westernization and Americanization, and, after undergoing this process, proceeds further to internationalization. A conception of this zig-zag process is important not only to America but to Japan as well, now and in the future. Twenty-five percent of Japan's exports in 1970 were shipped to developing nations in Asia other than the socialist-bloc nations, whereas Japan's imports from the same areas amounted to only 16 percent of her total imports. It is natural that criticism should arise against Japan's economic thrust, and we may regard this opposition as a manifestation of nationalism in Asia. Still, the majority of the Japanese today are not cognizant of this problem, and it is one with which they should be familiar in the process of improving education for Asia and Asian peoples.

It is difficult to deal with the problem of nationalism in Asia and Africa, since some areas are not full nation-states, but are still undergoing a process of formation. A point related to cultural interchange in this case is the phenomenon of the massive brain drain from Asia and Africa into America.

According to a National Science Foundation report (1972, p. 3) foreign scientists and technologists who emigrated to America in 1970 numbered 13,300, out of which 7,500 were from Asia and 1,000 from Africa. Compared to 1965, only five years earlier, the number had increased 14 times for Asia, and 20 times for Africa. The National Institutes of Health reported that in 1972, more than 1,500 physicians from India and slightly fewer than 800 from the Philippines emigrated to America. Emerging nations are desperately in need of physicians, scientists, and technologists, and the extent of the brain drain is a clear indication that the firm foundation necessary for proper functioning as a nation-state has yet to be realized in those countries. Under such circumstances, one is justified in anticipating that the dominant-subordinate relationship between developed industrial nations in the North and emerging nations in the South will continue.

Furthermore, one can expect that, within those emerging nations, conflicts will persist between those in power and those calling for a reformation of the social structure – as well as the concomitant confusions stemming from such conflicts.

International politics, as well as cultural interchange, should not intervene in the domestic affairs of other nations; however, in the long run, how will history unfold?

It should and will move in the direction wherein all nations equally maintain their respective positions and harmonize them with the solidarity of mankind. The path leading in this direction is thorny, but it will be cleared away gradually. It is natural that throughout my year in Hawaii, I reflected on these long-range perspectives.

In talking with students and faculty members at the East-West Center, I also suggested that if the United States desired to promote education about Asia, an emphasis must be placed on understanding such radical historical changes as the Meiji Restoration in Japan, the Hsin Hai Revolution in China, and socialist revolutions.

Another question with which I was concerned was the reexamination of the concept of "development." What attracted my attention to this problem was a remark made by Mrs. Patsy Mink, Congresswoman from Hawaii. She emphasized the importance of two-way communication between the United States and Asia instead of the present one-way transmission of American ideas and ideals to Asian areas.

When Mrs. Mink says, "Let's learn from Asia," she is proposing a departure from the so-called economic and technical cooperation (as well as the "exchange" of students) that has taken place to date, which has been characterized by a strong inclination to use the West or America as a model for the "development" or "elevation" of emerging areas. The terms *'developed nation,' 'developing nation,'* and *'underdeveloped area'* are testimony to the existence of this line of thinking in the cultural interchange and education of today.

Despite the fact that the East-West Center equalizes Asia and America in its name, America is considered a "developed nation" and Asia an "underdeveloped area." Accordingly, an underlying view at the center is that America in the North helps "developing" Asian nations in the South, and that the center is a place where the North-South problem is solved.

It is recognized that a common problem facing mankind is that of guaranteeing a satisfactory standard of living for emerging areas; yet are we justified in continuing with the long-accepted idea of "development"? Such thoughts were with me constantly during my year in Hawaii, especially when reflecting that the West, as represented by America, is now groping for a new set of values in the postindustrial age.

Jesus Christ, Superstar was recently performed in Tokyo by the Shiki, a theatrical group. It is relatively unknown, however, that, in parallel to this, students of the University of Hawaii and Pomona College in California have displayed an enthusiasm for Kabuki. The University of Hawaii scored a great hit in performing *Sukeroku* about two years ago, and last spring, they again created a sensation by presenting *Narukami*. (The reception was so enthusiastic that it was necessary to stage additional performances to satisfy overflowing audiences. Students assiduously portraying facets of traditional Japanese culture are in a way analogous to the presentation in Japan of Shakespearean drama, and I could not help but be moved deeply by the students' seriousness in undertaking such a project.)

The Industrial Revolution can be said to have sanctioned man's ever-expanding desire for production and consumption and to have given promise of the unlimitedness of these processes. American youth, who previously applauded the industrialized civilization, has come to doubt the basic premises on which that same civilization rests. In a speech at the East-West Center, Professor Harold Lasswell (1972) stated that what would become important in the future would be the level of maturity of the culture — that is, the quality rather than the quantity of life — and welfare rather than unrestricted, free competition in the economy.

Japan, along with America, is a "superior student" in the Pacific area in terms of GNP and per capita income; however, she is an "inferior student" from the standpoint of urban problems and environmental pollution. Thus a new problem in education should be how the so-called developed nations can be redeveloped with a new scale of values, rather than how they can "develop" other nations.

Another basic problem is that the globe is irreplaceable and limited in space. It may be said that the Industrial Revolution supported the notion of unlimitedness with the enthusiasm of whacking an "outside-the-stadium homer"; but we realize now that the only game our globe can afford is played within a limited arena.

Prohibition of nuclear weapons, security of resources and provisions, elimination of pollution, and restoration of nature — these are the problems that mankind has to solve. Education must seek the political, economic, and social systems that best enable man to achieve these objectives.

Given these conditions, one should not have a simplistic, romantic idea that education by itself can bring about great social changes without difficulties. One of the mistakes of radical students in the late 1960s was their belief that sharp criticism of higher education could lead naturally to great social changes. Even today, there are some who are inclined to think that such a position is tenable.

One of the reasons we see a larger number of a new type of student in place of radical students may be related to their realization of the difficulties of social reform. What is meant by "new type" is that group of students who may be characterized as belonging to the "counter-culture." They are not quite rebels against the present social structure; instead, they are moderate social disorganizers, but they have not yet come to a conclusion as to what would be the best culture and society necessary at the next stage of man's history.

The existence of such students is also an indication that changes will come probably more in the sphere of economy and politics than in the field of education. Many years ago, Hegel wrote:

To say one more word about preaching what the world ought to be like, philosophy arrives always too late for that. As *thought* of the world it appears at a time when actuality has completed its developmental process and is finished. What the conception teaches, history also shows as necessary, namely, that only in a maturing actuality the ideal appears and confronts the real. It is then that the ideal rebuilds for itself this same world in the shape of an intellectual realm, comprehending this world in its substance. When philosophy paints its gray in gray, a form of life has become old, and this gray in gray cannot rejuvenate it, only understand it. The owl of Minerva begins its flight when dusk is falling. (Hegel, 1820).

What education must do is to give people intellectual interpretations and directions when the real changes suddenly occur in the economy and politics. But when higher education is as highly developed as it is in the United States, one would not be too idealistic — in that society at least — if he were to expect the education of tomorrow to be an owl crying before dusk. In other words, if the field of education proceeds wisely, it will be able to foretell at least some of the coming changes in politics and the economy.

6. Some Proposals for the Future

We have arrived at a stage in world history when the more important and serious problems of every nation are becoming increasingly international and when only minor problems remain national. This trend is more obvious in the field of education than in any other. What I propose as directions for education in the United States, therefore, should also be applicable in my own country.

1. Organized skepticism — as characterized by Robert Merton — should be regarded as the first principle, not only of higher education, but of all education.

It must be taught, not from the freshman year of higher education, but from primary school. Although specialized knowledge and skills will remain important, skepticism will help to improve the relationship between the content of specialized education and the needs of the whole society. This will help to avoid, for example, pollution and the deterioration of the human environment. Skepticism also helps man to entertain a liberal and rich culture, the only basis from which man is able to contemplate the possible directions in which human society could be moving.

2 The education of tomorrow must be engaged in the exploration of the "inner frontier" of man.

If man could explore his inner frontier, he could caution himself against unnecessary idleness and could begin to find a meaning of life based on its quality rather than on that which is quantitatively measurable. To use the phraseology of David Riesman, we must nurture "the autonomous" in future education and society (Riesman, 1950).

Looking at the Japan of today, it is difficult to say whether we shall be able to control the strong influence of the mass media. According to a 1973 report of the Ministry of Posts and Telecommunications in the Japanese government, Japanese watch TV for an average of three hours and five minutes daily and devote only 30 minutes daily to reading the newspaper; furthermore, 90 percent of what they watch is entertainment. Although Japan today is boasting about its great development of mass communication, what this development means is that, first of all, the total population of Japan is spending an unbelievable amount of time-consuming, rather low-quality entertainment. The second shortcoming is a clear weakening of personal communication. In 1972, the number of pieces of mail in the country was 10 billion, of which 80 percent was used for business purposes. Japan is also known for the wide availability of the telephone; but here again, business utilized the telephone 5.5 times more than home users. The third drawback is that the sources of communication are concentrated more and more in the hands of business and the government. Like the mail and the telephone, technological facilities are increasingly utilized by larger business organizations rather than by individuals, and central and local governments are accumulating a large amount of information and spreading it by way of newspaper and TV (Yuseisho, 1974).

Under such circumstances, it is clear that despite the rapid growth of technological communication facilities, there is no question that the kind of information supplied to people is becoming increasingly homogeneous. I do not know any instant remedy for this unbalanced development of communication in Japan, and I am not in a position to assess the situation in the United States. One thing, however, seems to be certain: without making some special effort, the contemporary development of mass media will continue to foster what David Riesman called the "other directedness" of human character. In the long range, however, there might be some way of changing the character of mass media. This will be discussed later.

3. The content of education should be truly international.

Here, the United States obviously has spent more energy and has invested more than any other nation today to broaden the scope of education. As it was pointed out earlier, if there is any weakness, it is that internationalization has been sometimes misinterpreted by a sizeable number of Americans as synonymous with Americanization. It is a curious fact that although the United States comprises many races, it has, at the same time, built up a unified American culture. Japan is far more exclusive and nationalistic in terms of racial relations; as for its culture, however, it is difficult to say what the Japanese culture of today is. Most likely, it is a mixture of the Confucian, Buddhist, Shinto, and Western cultures. Both the United States and Japanese societies have merits, but their faults deserve more attention.

It will be necessary for the American people to study non-American languages and cultures and to learn the importance of nationalism as embraced by peoples of many different areas, especially those who belong to emerging nations. Nationalism will rise in many parts of the world, which older, industrialized nations must recognize. There also will be conflicts, not only among nations, but among races and religious groups in a given country. Such years could be characterized as years of somewhat militant struggle, and if we can avoid a large-scale war, an internationalism of a new kind will begin to emerge from the realization that the sufferings of man resulting from tension and conflict would be too costly and too hard to bear.

4. Liberal education must be reemphasized.

In spite of the repeated emphasis given by outstanding educators to the importance of liberal education, professional training and specialized research have become more and more important. It is a time for us to go back to the original plea for education in any great culture — that is, for the liberation of the mind of man.

In *The Academic Revolution,* Christopher Jencks and David Riesman (1968) wrote that there should be some reform in the graduate schools to design a strong curriculum for those who will teach in the field of liberal education to accord them an importance at least equal to those who teach in graduate and professional schools. This proposal is so important that we must consider how to build up such a curriculum.

One of the things Charles E. Silberman (1970) advocates in *Crisis in the Classroom* is to narrow the gap between journalism and formal school education. He came to this conviction on the basis of his personal experiences as a university professor and as an editorial writer for *Fortune* magazine. Having by chance shared the same past experiences as Silberman, I tend to think in the same way. Organized knowledge has been taught carefully, but it tends to become increasingly stagnant in a world where cultures and societies are very rapidly changing. It is necessary, therefore, to make school education more informal, meaning that there should be real contact between the content of education in schools and happenings in the larger society.

At the same time, there are some weaknesses in journalistic activities. They excel in reporting events of the world as quickly and as accurately as possible, but the kind of information that is supplied by the newspapers and TV is quite fragmented. Consequently, it is extremely difficult for the ordinary reader or viewer to derive any sense of historical context out of these fragmented bits of information. Journalism, therefore, should make a more courageous effort at editing news to clarify the alternative contexts of historical changes. Some may think such a new style of editing to be contrary to the journalistic principle of impartiality; as Max Weber (1949) made clear in *The Meth-*

odology of the Social Sciences, however, even the knowledge that is taught in schools cannot be totally impartial, and it is not wise to conceive of impartiality in a formalistic sense.

Max Weber also said that, in any research, the selection of problems for study and the formulation of a frame of reference are bound by relativistic historical perspectives. What is important in establishing the objectivity of knowledge is the ways in which study and research are carried out. To use his expression, "science is a logical conceptualization of reality." Logic that is universal and data that are empirically valid must be used for scientific studies. What Weber emphasizes in the *Methodology* is applicable to the activities of journalism. The editing of news, like research, is bound by relativistic historical perspectives in the selection of problems and in the formulation of intellectual frames of reference. Bearing these points clearly in mind, journalists should become more conscious of their role as transmitters of knowledge to readers and listeners. To put it more clearly, it would be ideal — and even necessary — to have classes from grade school on to the university where journalists themselves could go and teach, using newspapers and TV, about what they think to be the most important events of the world today. I know of no such course in a Japanese university, although there were some attempts of this kind in the middle schools right after World War II. I hope that such an experiment will be realized, not in Japan alone, but elsewhere in the world as well.

It would also be ideal if in-service training for teachers could break away from the classroom and require them to work in real society. It may not be necessary to make this requirement for those in all subject matters, but at least those in the fields of social science and the humanities would do well to move out of formal school education at times (as in sabbatical year) and become real workers of ongoing societies.

Having said this, I would propose that students themselves should not be confined to classrooms from nursery school on to graduate school. That is much too long a period for any person to be leaning to one side of human activity only. A study group of the Japan Teachers' Union has proposed that everyone should work for some period before he or she goes on to college, but this still is at the level of a proposal (*A Report of the Kyoiku Seido Kento Iinkai,* 1973).

Stephen Leacock (1949) wrote in an interesting book entitled *Toward Liberal Education* that field study encouraged by pragmatic philosophers could become too formalistic. He describes those students who, for the purpose of strengthening their work in social studies, go out to a department store and count the number of shoppers, thinking that is a true social study. As Socrates and other great philosophers of the past have suggested, deep thinking comes out of intellectual struggle in real life; to say that students must go out to the field does not mean that they should neglect the study of the great intellectual achievements of thinkers in the past.

Here, Robert Hutchins (1936) is undoubtedly right in his lifelong insistence that higher learning in America has tended to become too practical and that there should be more respect for a serious study of the classics during college life. What Hutchins said is also true with regard to the contents of liberal education in Japanese higher education. *Great Books of the West,* compiled by Robert Hutchins and Stringfellow Barr, are not easy to read; the same is true of the classics of the East. Though it is desirable that the classics are read at any moment in history, the need for their serious study is becoming acute today when we are at a turning point in world history and have nothing else but the accumulation of past knowledge to use as a tool to design the future shape of society and culture.

If great books are to have more value in the education of the future, so should the study of history. Higher education in the United States should pride itself on having produced more great scientists, engineers, and social scientists than the higher education of any other country. If I were to be somewhat courageous in expressing my assessment of the achievements of higher education in the United States, however, I would say that great historians have not been produced in the same proportion as those outstanding in the professions mentioned above; but this impression may be applicable not only to the United States but to all industrial societies of today. Again, if today is a turning point in history, the serious study of history by way of liberal education is that which invites young people to think about the directions in which they could and should be moving in the future.

5. The strength of the diversity of education, which is a part of the American tradition, must be encouraged.

There is no one absolute and sure way to the future. Intellectual experiments of all kinds must compete with one another to find better answers for the problems of mankind. One of the reports of the Carnegie Commission (Hodgkinson, 1971) pointed out that there has been a threat of homogenizing the content of higher education in recent years. Such a trend has been far more evident in Japan, where, in fact, there has been central planning by the government, and this, in my judgment, is one of the weakest points of Japanese education.

A teacher is able to teach well only when he teaches himself. A teacher who relies exclusively on another's knowledge can never encourage the creativity of students. Diversity of education means, in the final analysis, the initiative of every individual teacher to be engaged in creative teaching and research. This should be the enterprise of every department, every school, and the total school system of every country.

In the United States, large-scale, state-supported universities have become dominant, sometimes at the expense of small private colleges. In my view, the small private colleges have shown, more than the larger schools have, the importance of the creativity and diversity of education. As they have in Japan, most small private colleges in the United States have nearly lost their unique characteristics due to financial difficulties. Looking around the world today, a historical trend seems to be that educational institutions, including those of higher education, are increasingly financed by public funds in those societies where the welfare of all the people is becoming more and more important.

In the United States, therefore, a public policy of financing small but valuable educational experiments is desirable to maintain and strengthen the American tradition of diversity in education.

Another built-in merit of American society, in contrast to Japan, is that so many different races are living together. As anyone knows, the peaceful coexistence of different races and traditions in the same society is extremely difficult. Unless we overcome these difficulties in a nation like the United States, who could hope for the peaceful coexistence of the different ideologies, races, traditions, and nations of the world of tomorrow? Equality in the field of education should become more and more a reality regardless of race and tradition. Equality does not mean the homogenization of different traditions. All the nations of the world today must be internationalized year by year. Under such circumstances, the surest base for the internationalization of higher education in the United States lies in equal respect given to the different races and traditions within the country. Such an effort may be called a "new Americanization" in contrast to the traditional Americanization, which tended to be a kind of Westernization.

6. Solutions to global problems must be considered more and more seriously.

This was indicated by the survey on the thinking of young people mentioned in Chapter 1 and also in *Limits to Growth*, the report of the Club of Rome. All nations today share common problems, such as population, energy, resources, human environment, and arms control. It is an obligation of the more advanced nations of the world today to pour greater intellectual investment into possible solutions to these problems for the sake of mankind. Some people argue that there must be deeper concentration on the humanities and social studies for this purpose. Although this argument has some validity, it should not mean that a techno-scientific approach to these problems should be abandoned completely. Scientists and engineers must be engaged in their studies with the broader and deeper understanding of the human problems of today. In other words, the barrier between sciences and technology on the one hand and the humanities and social sciences on the other must be broken down in the higher education of tomorrow. It is easy to say this, of course, but the method to achieve such a goal will be new and very difficult. I do not know of any Japanese university in which a large-scale interdisciplinary approach includes all the branches of learning. The National Research Institute on Pollution, which started only in 1974, is aiming at such a new approach. I am sure that a similar trend will be embodied more frequently, not only in research institutions but also in universities and colleges elsewhere in the world.

Although there are many other problems in higher education today, including higher education in the United States, I have touched only upon those which seem to be vital. There are so many valuable studies as well as proposals for the reform of higher education in the United States that I am capable of setting forth for consideration here only limited general ideas; this is because my observation of higher education in the United States is that of a foreigner, and also because I am bound to be more involved in the questions of higher education in Japan. Indeed, what I have written in this essay with regard to higher education in the United States may be more applicable to higher education in Japan, for the latter, in my judgment, is in the midst of greater difficulties.

References

Ashby, Sir Eric: *Any Person, Any Study: An Essay on American Higher Education,* McGraw-Hill Book Company, New York, 1970.

Ben-David, Joseph: *American Education: Directions Old and New,* McGraw-Hill Book Company, New York, 1971

Benedict, Ruth: *The Chrysthanthemum and the Sword: Patterns of Japanese Culture,* Houghton Mifflin, Boston, 1946.

Cummings, William K.: "The Japanese Private University," *Minerva,* vol. 11, no. 3, July, 1973.

Glazer, Nathan: "Ethnicity and the Schools," *Commentary,* vol. 58, no. 3, September, 1971.

Hegel, George F.: "Philosophy of Right and Law," 1820, in *The Philosophy of Hegel,* Carl Friedrich, ed., Modern Library, New York, 1953.

Hodgkinson, Harold L.: *Institutions in Transition,* McGraw-Hill Book Company, New York, New York, 1971.

Hutchins, Robert: *Higher Learning in America,* McGraw-Hill Book Company, New York, 1936.

"Japanese Intellectuals — And Americans," *The American Scholar,* vol. 34, no. 1, Winter, 1964-65.

Jencks, Christopher, and David Riesman: *The Academic Revolution,* Doubleday and Co., New York, 1968.

Kawashima, Takeyoshi: *Nihon Shakai, no Kazokuteki Kosei* (Familistic Structure of Japanese Society), Nihon Hyoronsha, Tokyo, 1950.

Lasswell, Harold: "The Future of World Communication, Style and Quality of Life" (a paper read at the conference at the Communication Institute of the East-West Center, Hawaii, September, 1972 — unpublished).

Leacock, Stephen: "The New Education" in Louis G. Locke et al. eds., *Toward Liberal Education,* Rhinehart & Company, New York, 1949.

Maruyama, Masao: *Thought and Behaviour in Modern Japanese Politics,* Oxford University Press, London, 1963.

Meadows, Dennis L., and D. H. Meadows: *The Limits to Growth,* Universe Books, New York, 1972.

Merton, Robert: *Social Theory and Social Structure* (revised and enlarged edition), The Free Press, New York, 1964.

Nagai, Michio: *Shin Kyoiku Ron* (On New Education), Chuokoronsha, Tokyo, 1956.

Nagai, Michio: "Nihon o seou Tabi" (Self-conscious Journey as Japanese), in Soichi Oya, ed., *Sekai no Tabi* (Travel All Over the World), vol. 6, Chuokoronsha, Tokyo, 1962.

Nagai, Michio: *Higher Education in Japan,* University of Tokyo Press, Tokyo, 1971.

Nakane, Chie: *Human Relations in Japan,* Ministry of Foreign Affairs of Japan, Tokyo, 1972.

Parsons, Talcott: *The Social System,* The Free Press, New York, 1951.

Reeder, Ward G.: *Fundamentals of Public School Administration,* The Macmillan Company, New York, 1941.

Report of the Kyoiku Seido Kento Iinkai (Study Group on the Educational System), Tokyo, 1973.

Riesman, David: *The Lonely Crowd,* Yale University Press, New Haven, 1950.

Riesman, David and Evelyn Thompson Riesman: *Conversations in Japan: Modernization, Politics and Culture,* Basic Books, New York, 1967.

Samson, George B.: *Japan – A Short Cultural History,* Cresset Press, London, 1946.

Sengoku, Tomatsu and Atsuko Toyama: *Hikaku Nihonjin Ron* (A comparative Study of Japanese), Shogakukan, Tokyo, 1973.

Silberman, Charles E.: *Crisis in the Classroom,* Random House, New York, 1970.

Sorifu (Prime Minister's Office of Japan): *Sekai no Seinen Ishiki* (The Thinking of Young People of the World), July, 1973.

Touraine, Alain: *The Academic System in American Society,* McGraw-Hill Book Company, New York, 1974.

U.S. National Science Foundation: *Scientists, Engineers, and Physicians from Abroad, Trends Through Fiscal Year 1970,* Washington D.C., 1972.

U.S. Office of Education: *Digest of Educational Statistics,* Washington D.C., 1972.

Vogel, Ezra F.: *Japan's New Middle Class: A Salary Man and His Family in a Tokyo Suburb,* University of California Press, Berkeley, 1963.

Weber, Max: *The Methodology of the Social Sciences,* The Free Press, New York, 1949.

Yankelovich, Daniel: "Changing Youth Values in the Seventies: A Study of American Youth," March, 1974 (mimeographed).

Yuseisho (Japan Ministry of Communication), *Denki Tsushin no Genjo,* (Report on Electric Communication of Today), Tokyo, 1974.

Carnegie Commission on Higher Education

Sponsored Research Studies

The following publications are available from McGraw-Hill Book Company, Box 402, Hightstown, New Jersey, 08520.

THE DIVIDED ACADEMY:
PROFESSORS AND POLITICS
Everett Carll Ladd, Jr. and
Seymour Martin Lipset

EDUCATION AND POLITICS AT
HARVARD
Seymour Martin Lipset and
David Riesman

HIGHER EDUCATION AND EARNINGS:
COLLEGE AS AN INVESTMENT AND A
SCREENING DEVICE
Paul Taubman and Terence Wales

EDUCATION, INCOME, AND HUMAN
BEHAVIOR
F. Thomas Juster

AMERICAN LEARNED SOCIETIES
IN TRANSITION:
THE IMPACT OF DISSENT
AND RECESSION
Harland G. Bloland and
Sue M. Bloland

ANTIBIAS REGULATION OF
UNIVERSITIES: FACULTY PROBLEMS
AND THEIR SOLUTIONS
Richard A Lester

CHANGES IN UNIVERSITY
ORGANIZATION, 1964-1971
Edward Gross and Paul V. Grambsch

ESCAPE FROM THE DOLL'S HOUSE:
WOMEN IN GRADUATE AND
PROFESSIONAL SCHOOL EDUCATION
Saul D. Feldman

THE ACADEMIC SYSTEM
IN AMERICAN SOCIETY
Alain Touraine

HIGHER EDUCATION
AND THE LABOR MARKET
Margaret S. Gordon (ed.)

THE ACADEMIC MELTING POT:
CATHOLICS AND JEWS IN
AMERICAN HIGHER EDUCATION
Stephen Steinberg

LEADERSHIP AND AMBIGUITY:
THE AMERICAN COLLEGE PRESIDENT
Michael D. Cohen and James G. March

CONTENT AND CONTEXT:
ESSAYS ON COLLEGE EDUCATION
Carl Kaysen (ed.)

EDUCATION FOR THE PROFESSIONS
OF MEDICINE, LAW, THEOLOGY, AND
SOCIAL WELFARE
*Everett C. Hughes, Barrie Thorne,
Agostino M. DeBaggis, Arnold Gurin, and
David Williams*

T HE FUTURE OF HIGHER EDUCATION:
SOME SPECULATIONS AND SUGGESTIONS
Alexander M. Mood

THE RISE OF THE ARTS
ON THE AMERICAN CAMPUS
Jack Morrison

THE UNIVERSITY AND THE CITY:
EIGHT CASES OF INVOLVEMENT
*George Nash, Dan Waldorf,
and Robert E. Price*

THE BEGINNING OF THE FUTURE: A
HISTORICAL APPROACH TO GRADUATE
EDUCATION IN THE ARTS AND SCIENCES
Richard J. Storr

ACADEMIC TRANSFORMATION:
SEVENTEEN INSTITUTIONS UNDER
PRESSURE
David Riesman and Verne A. Stadtman (eds.)

THE UNIVERSITY AS AN ORGANIZATION
James A. Perkins (ed.)

WHERE COLLEGES ARE AND
WHO ATTENDS:
EFFECTS OF ACCESSIBILITY ON
COLLEGE ATTENDANCE
*C. Arnold Anderson, Mary Jean
Bowman and Vincent Tinto*

THE EMERGING TECHNOLOGY:
INSTRUCTIONAL USE OF THE
COMPUTER IN HIGHER
EDUCATION
Roger E. Levien

NEW DIRECTIONS IN LEGAL
EDUCATION
Herbert L. Packer and Thomas Ehrlich

A STATISTICAL PORTRAIT OF
HIGHER EDUCATION
Seymour E. Harris

EDUCATION AND EVANGELISM:
A PROFILE OF PROTESTANT COLLEGES
C. Robert Pace

THE HOME OF SCIENCE:
THE ROLE OF THE UNIVERSITY
Dael Wolfle

PROFESSIONAL EDUCATION:
SOME NEW DIRECTIONS
Edgar H. Schein

THE NONPROFIT RESEARCH
INSTITUTE: ITS ORIGIN, OPERATION,
PROBLEMS, AND PROSPECTS
Harold Orlans

THE INVISIBLE COLLEGES:
A PROFILE OF SMALL, PRIVATE
COLLEGES WITH LIMITED RESOURCES
Alexander W. Astin and Calvin B. T. Lee

AMERICAN HIGHER EDUCATION:
DIRECTIONS OLD AND NEW
Joseph Ben-David

A DEGREE AND WHAT ELSE?:
CORRELATES AND CONSEQUENCES OF
A COLLEGE EDUCATION
*Stephen B. Withey, Jo Anne Coble, Gerald
Gurin, John P. Robinson, Burkhard Strumpel,
Elizabeth Keogh Taylor, and Arthur C. Wolfe*

THE MULTICAMPUS UNIVERSITY:
A STUDY OF ACADEMIC GOVERNANCE
Eugene C. Lee and Frank M. Bowen

INSTITUTIONS IN TRANSITION:
A PROFILE OF CHANGE IN HIGHER
EDUCATION
(INCORPORATING THE 1970
STATISTICAL REPORT)
Harold L. Hodgkinson

EFFICIENCY IN LIBERAL EDUCATION:
A STUDY OF COMPARATIVE INSTRUC-
TIONAL COSTS FOR DIFFERENT WAYS
OF ORGANIZING TEACHING-LEARNING
IN A LIBERAL ARTS COLLEGE
Howard R. Bowen and Gordon K. Douglass

CREDIT FOR COLLEGE:
PUBLIC POLICY FOR STUDENT LOANS
Robert W. Hartman

MODELS AND MAVERICKS:
A PROFILE OF PRIVATE LIBERAL
ARTS COLLEGES
Morris T. Keeton

BETWEEN TWO WORLDS:
A PROFILE OF NEGRO HIGHER
EDUCATION
Frank Bowles and Frank A. DeCosta

BREAKING THE ACCESS BARRIERS:
A PROFILE OF TWO-YEAR COLLEGES
Leland L. Medsker and Dale Tillery

ANY PERSON, ANY STUDY:
AN ESSAY ON HIGHER EDUCATION IN
THE UNITED STATES
Eric Ashby

THE NEW DEPRESSION IN HIGHER
EDUCATION:
A STUDY OF FINANCIAL CONDITIONS
AT 41 COLLEGES AND UNIVERSITIES
Earl F. Cheit

FINANCING MEDICAL EDUCATION:
AN ANALYSIS OF ALTERNATIVE
POLICIES AND MECHANISMS
Rashi Fein and Gerald I. Weber

HIGHER EDUCATION IN NINE
COUNTRIES:
A COMPARATIVE STUDY OF COLLEGES
AND UNIVERSITIES ABROAD
*Barbara B. Burn, Philip G. Altbach, Clark
Kerr, and James A. Perkins*

BRIDGES TO UNDERSTANDING:
INTERNATIONAL PROGRAMS OF AMER-
ICAN COLLEGES AND UNIVERSITIES
Irwin T. Sanders and Jennifer C. Ward

GRADUATE AND PROFESSIONAL
EDUCATION, 1980:
A SURVEY OF INSTITUTIONAL PLANS
Lewis B. Mayhew
*(Out of print, but available from
University Microfilms.)*

THE AMERICAN COLLEGE AND
AMERICAN CULTURE:
SOCIALIZATION AS A FUNCTION OF
HIGHER EDUCATION
Oscar Handlin and Mary F. Handlin

RECENT ALUMNI AND HIGHER
EDUCATION:
A SURVEY OF COLLEGE GRADUATES
Joe L. Spaeth and Andrew M. Greeley

CHANGE IN EDUCATIONAL POLICY:
SELF-STUDIES IN SELECTED COLLEGES
AND UNIVERSITIES
Dwight R. Ladd

STATE OFFICIALS AND HIGHER
EDUCATION:
A SURVEY OF THE OPINIONS AND
EXPECTATIONS OF POLICY MAKERS IN
NINE STATES
Heinz Eulau and Harold Quinley
*(Out of print, but available from
University Microfilms.)*

ACADEMIC DEGREE STRUCTURES:
INNOVATIVE APPROACHES
PRINCIPLES OF REFORM IN DEGREE
STRUCTURES IN THE UNITED STATES
Stephen H. Spurr

COLLEGES OF THE FORGOTTEN
AMERICANS:
A PROFILE OF STATE COLLEGES
AND REGIONAL UNIVERSITIES
E. Alden Dunham

FROM BACKWATER TO MAINSTREAM:
A PROFILE OF CATHOLIC HIGHER
EDUCATION
Andrew M. Greeley

THE ECONOMICS OF THE MAJOR
PRIVATE UNIVERSITIES
William G. Bowen
*(Out of print, but available from
University Microfilms.)*

THE FINANCE OF HIGHER EDUCATION
Howard R. Bowen
*(Out of print, but available from
University Microfilms.)*

ALTERNATIVE METHODS OF FEDERAL
FUNDING FOR HIGHER EDUCATION
Ron Wolk
*(Out of print, but available from
University Microfilms.)*

INVENTORY OF CURRENT RESEARCH
ON HIGHER EDUCATION 1968
Dale M. Heckman and Warren Bryan Martin
*(Out of print, but available from
University Microfilms.)*

*The following technical reports are available from the Carnegie Commission on
Higher Education, 2150 Shattuck Avenue, Berkeley, California 94704.*

AN OWL BEFORE DUSK
Michio Nagai

THE GREAT AMERICAN DEGREE
MACHINE: AN ECONOMIC ANALYSIS
OF HUMAN RESOURCE OUTPUT OF
HIGHER EDUCATION
Douglas L. Adkins

The following reprints are available from the Carnegie Commission on Higher Education, 2150 Shattuck Avenue, Berkeley, California 94704. (First copies of reprints are sent free on request. Enclose 20 cents each for additional copies to defray costs of postage and handling.)

PROBLEMS IN THE TRANSITION FROM ELITE TO MASS HIGHER EDUCATION, by Martin Trow. A paper prepared for a conference on mass higher education sponsored by the Organisation for Economic Co-operation and Development, June 1973.

MEASURING FACULTY UNIONISM: QUANTITY AND QUALITY, by Bill Aussieker and J. W. Garbarino, reprinted from INDUSTRIAL RELATIONS, vol. 12, no. 2, May 1973.

COMING OF MIDDLE AGE IN HIGHER EDUCATION, by Earl F. Cheit, address delivered to American Association of State Colleges and Universities and National Association of State Universities and Land-Grant Colleges, Washington, D.C., November 13, 1972.

THE DISTRIBUTION OF ACADEMIC TENURE IN AMERICAN HIGHER EDUCATION, by Martin Trow, reprinted from Bardwell Smith (ed.) THE TENURE DEBATE, Jossey-Bass, San Francisco, 1972.

THE NATURE AND ORIGINS OF THE CARNEGIE COMMISSION ON HIGHER EDUCATION, by Alan Pifer, based on a speech delivered to the Pennsylvania Association of Colleges and Universities, Oct. 16, 1972, reprinted by permission of The Carnegie Foundation for the Advancement of Teaching.

MORE FOR LESS: HIGHER EDUCATION'S NEW PRIORITY, by Virginia B. Smith, reprinted from UNIVERSAL HIGHER EDUCATION: COSTS AND BENEFITS, American Council on Education, Washington, D.C., 1971. *

ACADEMIA AND POLITICS IN AMERICA, by Seymour M. Lipset, reprinted from Thomas J. Nossiter (ed.), IMAGINATION AND PRECISION IN THE SOCIAL SCIENCES, pp. 211-289, Faber and Faber, London, 1972. *

POLITICS OF ACADEMIC NATURAL SCIENTISTS AND ENGINEERS, by Everett C. Ladd, Jr., and Seymour M. Lipset. reprinted from Science, vol. 176, no. 4039, pp. 1091-1100, June 9, 1972.

THE INTELLECTUAL AS CRITIC AND REBEL: WITH SPECIAL REFERENCE TO THE UNITED STATES AND THE SOVIET UNION, by Seymour M. Lipset and Richard B. Dobson, reprinted from DAEDALUS, vol. 101, no. 3, pp. 137-198, Summer 1972.

POLITICS OF AMERICAN SOCIOLOGISTS by Seymour M. Lipset and Everett C. Ladd, Jr., reprinted from AMERICAN JOURNAL OF SOCIOLOGY, vol. 78, no. 1, pp. 67-104, July 1972.

FACULTY UNIONISM: FROM THEORY TO PRACTICE, by Joseph W. Garbarino, reprinted from INDUSTRIAL RELATIONS, vol. 11, no. 1, pp. 1-17, February 1972. *

INTERNATIONAL PROGRAMS OF U.S. COLLEGES AND UNIVERSITIES: PRIORITIES FOR THE SEVENTIES, by James A. Perkins, Occasional Paper No. 1, July 1971, reprinted by permission of the International Council for Education Development. *

ACCELERATED PROGRAMS OF MEDICAL EDUCATION, by Mark S. Blumberg, reprinted from JOURNAL OF MEDICAL EDUCATION, vol. 46, no. 8, August 1971. *

SCIENTIFIC MANPOWER FOR 1970-1985, *by Allan M. Cartter, reprinted from* SCIENCE, *vol. 172, no. 3979, pp. 132-140, April 9, 1971.* *

A NEW METHOD OF MEASURING STATES' HIGHER EDUCATION BURDEN, *by Neil Timm, reprinted from* THE JOURNAL OF HIGHER EDUCATION, *vol. 42, no. 1, pp. 27-33, January 1971.* *

REGENT WATCHING, *by Earl F. Cheit, reprinted from* AGB REPORTS, *vol. 13, no. 6, pp. 4-13, March 1971.* *

COLLEGE GENERATIONS—FROM THE 1930's TO THE 1960's, *by Seymour M. Lipset and Everett C. Ladd, Jr., reprinted from* THE PUBLIC INTEREST, *no. 24, Summer 1971.* *

AMERICAN SOCIAL SCIENTISTS AND THE GROWTH OF CAMPUS POLITICAL ACTIVISM IN THE 1960's, *by Everett C. Ladd, Jr., and Seymour M. Lipset, reprinted from* SOCIAL SCIENCES INFORMATION, *vol. 10, no. 2, April 1971.*

THE POLITICS OF AMERICAN POLITICAL SCIENTISTS, *by Everett C. Ladd, Jr., and Seymour M. Lipset, reprinted from PS, vol. 4, no. 2, Spring 1971.* *

THE DIVIDED PROFESSORIATE, *by Seymour M. Lipset and Everett C. Ladd, Jr., reprinted from CHANGE, vol. 3, no. 3, pp. 54-60, May 1971.* *

JEWISH ACADEMICS IN THE UNITED STATES: THEIR ACHIEVEMENTS, CULTURE AND POLITICS, *by Seymour M. Lipset and Everett C. Ladd, Jr., reprinted from* AMERICAN JEWISH YEAR BOOK, *1971.* *

THE UNHOLY ALLIANCE AGAINST THE CAMPUS, *by Kenneth Keniston and Michael Lerner, reprinted from* NEW YORK TIMES MAGAZINE, *November 8, 1970.* *

PRECARIOUS PROFESSORS: NEW PATTERNS OF REPRESENTATION, *by Joseph W. Garbarino, reprinted from* INDUSTRIAL RELATIONS, *vol. 10, no. 1, February 1971.* *

...AND WHAT PROFESSORS THINK: ABOUT STUDENT PROTEST AND MANNERS, MORALS, POLITICS, AND CHAOS ON THE CAMPUS, *by Seymour Martin Lipset and Everett Carll Ladd, Jr., reprinted from* PSYCHOLOGY TODAY, *November 1970.* *

DEMAND AND SUPPLY IN U.S. HIGHER EDUCATION: A PROGRESS REPORT, *by Roy Radner and Leonard S. Miller, reprinted from* AMERICAN ECONOMIC REVIEW, *May 1970.* *

RESOURCES FOR HIGHER EDUCATION: AN ECONOMIST'S VIEW, *by Theodore W. Schultz, reprinted from* JOURNAL OF POLITICAL ECONOMY, *vol. 76, no. 3, University of Chicago, May/June 1968.* *

INDUSTRIAL RELATIONS AND UNIVERSITY RELATIONS, *by Clark Kerr, reprinted from* PROCEEDINGS OF THE 21ST ANNUAL WINTER MEETING OF THE INDUSTRIAL RELATIONS RESEARCH ASSOCIATION, *pp. 15-25.* *

NEW CHALLENGES TO THE COLLEGE AND UNIVERSITY, *by Clark Kerr, reprinted from Kermit Gordon (ed.),* AGENDA FOR THE NATION, *The Brookings Institution, Washington, D.C., 1968.* *

PRESIDENTIAL DISCONTENT, *by Clark Kerr, reprinted from David C. Nichols (ed.),* PERSPECTIVES ON CAMPUS TENSIONS: PAPERS PREPARED FOR THE SPECIAL COMMITTEE ON CAMPUS TENSIONS, *American Council on Education, Washington, D.C., September 1970.* *

STUDENT PROTEST–AN INSTITUTIONAL AND NATIONAL PROFILE, *by Harold Hodgkinson, reprinted from* THE RECORD, *vol. 71, no. 4, May 1970.* *

WHAT'S BUGGING THE STUDENTS? *by Kenneth Keniston, reprinted from* EDUCATIONAL RECORD, *American Council on Education, Washington, D.C., Spring 1970.* *

THE POLITICS OF ACADEMIA, *by Seymour Martin Lipset, reprinted from David C. Nichols (ed.),* PERSPECTIVES ON CAMPUS TENSIONS: PAPERS PREPARED FOR THE SPECIAL COMMITTEE ON CAMPUS TENSIONS, *American Council on Education, Washington, D.C., September 1970.* *